The Grim Reapers

At Work in the Pacific Theater

The Third Attack Group
of the U.S. Fifth Air Force

The Grim Reapers

At Work in the Pacific Theater

The Third Attack Group
of the U.S. Fifth Air Force

John P. Henebry

Major General USAF, Retired

Library of Congress
Control Number 2002111049

ISBN 1-57510-093-2

First Printing October 2002

PRINTED IN CANADA

Cover Painting
Michael Hagel

Typography, Book and Cover Design
Arrow Graphics
with
Four Stars Media

Published by Pictorial Histories Publishing Company, Inc.
713 South Third Street West, Missoula, Montana 59801

Contents

Note from the Author

I have published this book, primarily about my active combat years in the Army Air Corps during World War II, to relate the extraordinary effort, determination, ability, and bravery shown by the individuals with whom I was associated throughout those years.

The results of the successes we achieved in accomplishing our military objectives in the Southwest Pacific advanced the concept of General George Kenney that we should use air surveillance, cover, and attack both on land and at sea.

I hope you will honor all of the servicemen and women who dedicated their lives to the freedom of the United States and the rest of the world. Too many gave their lives so that we may remain free.

Appreciation

I thank Mary Grey Kaye for working with me, deciphering my many hard-to-read notes, and spending the long hours with the recordings of the stories by Doc Gilmore and me about the unfolding history of the events of World War II in the Southwest Pacific. Your editing of the chronology of the advances of the Third Attack Group and the powerfully executed plans to end the aggressions and the war has created a continuity so that the reader may better understand the dynamics of the times and situations.

Also, thanks to John Cloe, Chief of History of the Third Wing at Elmendorf Air Force Base in Alaska, for checking and supplying the details of the book as it unfolded and suggesting various photographs to more vividly bring to life moments of the war in the Southwest Pacific.

The cover jacket of the book is a copy of the painting "Simpson Harbor" by Michael Hagel, which brings to you the feeling of the battle and the risks that each of us faced with every combat mission. Thank you, Mike, for allowing all of our airmen to be remembered with such a dramatic painting.

Finally, to my dear friend, Doc Gilmore, thank you for adding so much color and detail to the many events in which we participated throughout those years. Your counsel and vision were key elements to the success of the Third Attack Group. Doc, you are a true friend.

Dedication

I dedicate this book to my children, Patricia, John, Walter, Mary and Jeannine, and their mother, Mary McGuire Henebry.

I also keep in my heart my mother and father, Hanna and Joseph Henebry, who allowed me to follow my dreams.

Finally, the friends and fellow military personnel, those named and unnamed, are reflected in my memory, admiration, respect, and appreciation for their commitment and dedication to our country.

Preface

JOHN E. GILMORE, COLONEL USAF, RETIRED

THE Australian war correspondent scurried out of the belly of the B-25. The bomber's wheels had barely touched the tarmac at the Brisbane airport when the excited reporter was radioing his newspaper that a speed record surely had been broken on the run from Sydney.

More amazing than the air speed, according to the correspondent, was the dawn takeoff from Sydney's Mascot Airdrome with Major John "Jock" Henebry deftly piloting the plane. As he roared down the harbor, the magnificent sprawling Harbor Bridge loomed before him—a challenging sight. With daredevil instinct and a nod to his co-pilot, Jock took the plane down to 50 feet and cleared not only the underside of the bridge but a loaded ferry boat carrying workers to their jobs in town.

The B-25 was the "Fat Cat," the Third Attack Group's stripped-down Mitchell bomber, a creation of Captain John "Robbie" Robinson's engineering section,

John Henebry in the cockpit of "Fat Cat"

which was built from three wrecked B-25s and used for R & R runs between New Guinea and Australia during World War II. This flight was filled, as was the norm, with war-related personnel hitching a ride north, the correspondent among them. Henebry was a newly appointed squadron commander of the Third Attack Group, currently busy pushing Japanese up and off the north coast of New Guinea. The "Fat Cat" and Henebry had both been seasoned by more than a year of fierce and continuous Southwest Pacific air battles.

Brisbane had been their gassing stop before Port Moresby, on the south coast of New Guinea, with Dobodura their final destination, Henebry's northern New Guinea home base beyond the Owen Stanley mountain range.

Brisbane was also Douglas MacArthur's general headquarters—an unfortunate combination of person, place and event. For, waiting at Port Moresby as the plane taxied in, was General George Kenney, the theater's top air officer, with a TWX from MacArthur relaying orders to destripe this pilot upon arrival. There were no secrets in wartime Brisbane.

By this time in the Pacific theater, the Third Attack Group had become the point force in Kenney's increasingly successful air attack strategies and Henebry was a warrior, one of the best combat pilots in the air. So, waving the telegraphed sheet, Kenney reluctantly announced to the emerging pilot, "I have this order from MacArthur to break you—to take you down, down to buck private. Now I've got to do something so I'm going to give you an administrative reprimand but you get that goddamn airplane across the mountains before any other messages reach me. Get the hell out of here. Get back into the fight."

That is Doc Gilmore's story. Doc, Jock's war buddy, was Flight Surgeon for the Third and sitting in the co-pilot seat of the "Fat Cat" on this nerve-rattling flight. Jock denies some of the story, but the following stories he does admit to of the air war against the Japanese—a war he joined six months after Pearl Harbor and stayed with until the peace was signed aboard the battleship *Missouri*.

John Henebry returning to Sydney in 1990s for remembrance

1

Jenny

THE silence in the cockpit, the stillness of the volcanoes, the quiet over the
harbor, the steady mesmerizing drone of the B-25s gave us the moment
to take our last deep breath before we plunged into battle. Nothing before
me but Japanese ships. Behind me, the largest mass of Allied airplanes yet sent
against this unrelenting enemy.

The date was November 2, 1943. The mission was Rabaul. The Third Attack
Group led it and, as Group Operations Officer, I planned the course and led
our Group. Eleven squadrons of the Fifth Air Force followed us.

Two minutes later, after a 500-feet-per-second roller coaster flight, down on
a freighter transport, machine gunning the deck and skipping a bomb into her
side, vaulting the mast and down again on another freighter, more machine gunning,
another bomb, then hurdling another mast, I was belly up to the anti-aircraft
guns of a Japanese man-o'-war. The battle was over for me.

They shot up my rudder and knocked out the rear turret guns. A Japanese
fighter plane smelled the blood and jumped us, taking out our left engine. After
the cool of the two-and-a-half-hour flight from Port Moresby, the rush of the
attack now gave way to my wondering, "What—the hell—am I doing—here?"

To say that this thunderous aviation career started at age 12 in the bathroom of
my Plainfield, Illinois home seems a dramatic simplification, but the fact is, it did.

One summer afternoon, probably in 1930 as close as I can recall, I was
upstairs brushing my teeth when I heard a sound I had never heard before in real
life. I recognized it from movies and radio. Here it was, close by—an airplane.
Sure enough.

I scrambled out the second floor window onto the roof of our back porch and
saw the plane as it turned to make a pass over the field behind our back property.
We lived on the south edge of a farm town and the pilot evidently was looking
over the newly harvested wheat field as a possible landing site. He then made

another low pass over the next field beyond. It was a little larger, about 40 acres, and must have seemed better for his purpose. He continued his low pass and disappeared below a hedge row, not to reappear. The engine stopped. He had landed.

My brother and some neighborhood kids were already in the back yard watching the phenomenon as I caught sight of it from the roof. None of us could believe it—an airplane in Plainfield.

The landing demanded immediate inspection. We jumped on our always-at-the-ready bikes and started for the field where we figured he had put down.

As we hit the street, a fleet of bikes—more bikes than I realized our neighborhood harbored—was forming up rapidly. We rode two blocks east to get to the main road that led south out of town. It became a race. It would have been a matter of great honor and distinction to be the first cyclist to lay eyes on the first airplane in Plainfield. I didn't win the race, I would remember that victory if I had, but I wasn't far behind the kid who did.

We sped about a half a mile down the farm road to find that the pilot had just parked by a fence in a freshly cut wheat field. He was climbing out of the rear cockpit of a single engine, bi-winged World War I Curtiss "Jenny" as our horde descended upon him.

The pilot has no name in my memory but the looks of him are vivid in my mind still. He was as we would anticipate from the WWI and movie posters we had seen over the years: alone, wearing a flying helmet and goggles, a leather jacket, puttees and boots. His face was weather-beaten and he limped as he moved away from the plane.

Plainfield had produced no WWI pilots but we did have our share of war veterans who had been overseas, many of whom followed the bicycle brigade to the wheat field in a parade of Chevys and Fords. Other townspeople joined the children and the vets in the gathering crowd.

Because there were no pilots among the sightseers, the vets served as an ad hoc welcoming committee. They could talk WWI lingo. I recall someone asking this newly arrived stranger how he came by the limp and he used some French names to describe where he was when his hip was shot up. It may have been Chateau-Thierry or Amiens.

The pilot stayed around town for a few days following his landing, working on the plane's motor and exterior under our steady surveillance. He could carry two passengers in the front cockpit and offered rides at five dollars per passenger.

Naturally I had visions of being in that front cockpit during a flight, but the five dollar fare was astronomical to this newspaper carrier, delivering mornings and evenings, Mondays through Sundays, clearing $3.25 to $3.75 a week.

But had it been only a nickel, judging from the discussions around the dinner table, my mother and dad were not prone to give me clearance.

One morning the plane and our imported local hero were gone. We never knew where he came from nor where he went. But the vision of him swooping down on that freshly mowed field, living an unhindered life among strangers as he introduced them to the skies, pocketing some money in the process, being their immediate and undisputed hero, and then, free like the birds he emulated, moving on to other pastures as spirit and necessity dictated stayed in my soul. I couldn't know then in my child's mind what problems this pilot most likely encountered—merely keeping the old Jenny afloat probably being his major concern. I would certainly have traded my paper route for his life.

Notre Dame, "My" Lady

THE first compelling image of the University of Notre Dame is of its Golden Dome. Most who visit see it reaching into the sky. When I first came to that campus as a student in September 1936, I saw the sky sitting on the dome. I wanted to be in that sky, beyond that dome.

Five years after entering the university, I was up there, piloting a B-25—the Mighty Mitchell.

I followed my brother, Joe, to Notre Dame. The family goal was for us to acquire educations and degrees. I recall no other discussion about our futures beyond that achievement.

Aviation had stayed in my mind through my growing years, but not in the category of career. Plainfield had scant aviation activity. The closest airport was a grass strip over in Joliet, several miles away. Our family cars were not available to me nor my brother, Joe, for jaunts around town much less to bring me to the airstrip. After our flurry of activity when that barnstormer and his Jenny touched down, I had little exposure to airplanes or airfields to fuel my dreams. Career aviators were stunt pilots, distance pilots and racers. None of the above were the paths my father was driving us to South Bend to follow. His ambitions for his sons became more embedded after his accidental death the summer after my freshman year.

Two years into Notre Dame, the Army Air Corps reignited those dreams of youth again with information of its Flying Cadet Program open to juniors able to pass Army examinations. Now a widow, my mother's intense determination that I continue on to a Notre Dame graduation put another halt to any movement I could make toward a life in aviation.

However, the next year my Uncle Ed Blair and my cousin Dick came to campus to visit me and we three went over to the South Bend Airport where the pilot of a Gull Wing Stenson was offering rides. Finally, my first airplane ride. I was 20. I was hooked.

John Henebry after his first plane ride in 1939

At the same time the government offered its Civil Aeronautics Administration (CAA) Pilot Training Program through civilian airports. The local program was available at government expense at a fixed base operation at the South Bend airport with Homer Stockert in charge of flight instruction. With a minimum of family discussion, Homer had become my instructor by the winter of my senior year.

On campus, Notre Dame's Engineering Department supplied the ground school courses for the CAA program. I signed up for all that were offered—navigational problems, theory on aerodynamics, meteorology, fundamentals of aircraft and engine engineering. The courses were basic and designed to support the Pilot Training Program. They offered a solid foundation. I added these studies to the requirements of my business major curriculum.

It was a heavy, rewarding, serious year.

About a dozen of us, half of them fellow Domers, flew throughout the school year, including vacations. By the following summer I had 35 hours in the air and my student pilot's license, good for single engine flying. That license was more satisfying than my business degree, as my final year's grades might indicate.

More importantly, I was flying without becoming airsick. I threw up my first five times in the air with Homer, who comforted me with the observation that "people have reacted like this before and they often are able to get over it." So I stuck with flying in spite of the initial need to have a bag with me at all times, or in worse cases, to open up the side hatch and "let her fly." I did cut a couple of the lessons short but eventually, as promised and with Homer's constant consolation, overcame airsickness. Never, in the subsequent years of flying, have I heaved.

Military planes were a rare sight during my years at South Bend as we sat out the European turmoil. The nearby Bendix Corporation, a supplier of military parts and equipment, brought an occasional Army Air Corps plane into the area. I would see B-17s, four-engine flying fortresses that became so popular in World War II, flying into the local airport. They were the largest operational airplane of its kind and distinctive in their size. A flight of P-36s, Army Air Corps pursuit planes, once came in for a landing and then took off. I longingly watched them join together in formation as they left the area.

These incidental sightings drew me unwaveringly to the military. I was the only one in my class so inclined, the only graduate to go into uniform directly from graduation. It was a period of general disinterest in war among the young.

Not me. As the CAA training was finalizing with its imminent pilot's license, I had applied for an appointment to the Army Air Corps Flying Cadet Program.

Preliminary to the appointment was an Air Corps physical exam administered at Chanute Field near Champaign, Illinois. I failed it. I failed because of excessive esophoria—a slight weakness in the eye muscles that tends to turn the eye inward or outward when it becomes tired. Only technical equipment could detect the problem. The standard was later minimized in military pilot physicals because it had proved to be meaningless.

I went quickly for a second opinion from the Eye Department at the Woodruff Clinic in nearby Joliet. Dr. Woodruff himself understood the Air Corps diagnosis but didn't agree that it was a disabling weakness. He found nothing seriously wrong with my eyes and recommended eye exercises to strengthen the involved muscles to ready me for re-testing. He set me up with a therapy program involving a lighted candle and a series of prisms that I took back to my dorm room at Notre Dame.

Every day through the remaining months of my senior year I spent all available time looking at a lighted candle through a series of hand held prescription lenses exercising and strengthening the muscles of my eyes. The ritual became a constant basis of ribbing from my roommate and other residents of Sorin Hall.

Then, when a traveling Air Corps medical examination team returned to the university, I went through another complete exam including another eye test, and passed. Dr. Woodruff's therapy had worked.

I was judged fit. My college degree was close at hand, the year was 1940 and my future seemed clear.

The day after my July graduation, with my flying cadet appointment, I reported to the Federal Building in Chicago. There, I raised my right hand in an oath and with that was in the Army Air Corps.

That same day I emerged from the Federal Building and headed for the train station with a top coat and a toothbrush. Destination: Tulsa, Oklahoma, for primary flying school. I was on a regular commercial train, departing Chicago, changing trains in Kansas City, heading west for the Spartan School of Aeronautics, contractors to the Army Air Corps to provide military flight training.

I think often of that afternoon in Chicago with my widowed mother saying a difficult goodbye to a son taking up aviation and the military—both strange worlds to her. It was a mysterious life stretching before both of us.

Entering Spartan was one of the turning points of my life. My life as I wanted to live it really began for me that summer day in 1940. I met fellows approximately my age, from all over the United States, some of them with no college education, some of them with a couple years of college and some of us with baccalaureates, in addition to 18 second lieutenants from the West Point graduating class of 1940. The college degrees did give a jump start to those who held them and I was grateful now to my mother, who pushed me toward graduation through all those years when all I wanted was wings.

The studies and flight training at Tulsa were well run. Military officers and non-commissioned officers supervised the military training and oversaw the academics and flight training. We were flying the Stearman PT-17—a single engine biplane, fabric covered, stable, good for aerobatics. A great primary trainer.

I never had a military flight instructor. All were civilians. The stock of military

John Henebry during basic flight training school at Randolph Field, Texas in 1940

pilots coming out of World War I with combat experience was not large enough to supply instructors for our expanding air personnel. Military combat flyers did give lectures, reports and debriefings. How thoroughly I learned.

The ground schooling was quite extensive and rigorous. I moved through the four months of Primary Training with focus. Some 250 of us, less than half of those who started with me, were graduated. The rest washed out as pilots but many were offered the opportunity to go on to navigation or bombardier training.

Washouts were on a quota system. We were at the mercy of numbers. The Air Corps required a predetermined quantity of pilots moving through training to guarantee a set number of graduates. While this system methodically shaved the larger numbers originally admitted to flying school, the threat of brutal washout kept our attention level high. After that first cut the washout rate diminished dramatically.

In September 1940, the 40 percent of us who made it through Primary Flight Training were transferred down to Randolph Field at San Antonio, Texas, for Basic Flight Training where we flew the PT-14. Randolph Field was "The West Point of the Air" according to the signboard at the entrance.

Here we accumulated experience in aerobatics. We had already proven a basic ability to fly. Here we got good at fighter piloting, attack piloting. We learned to suck in our chins and guts, throw our shoulders back. We learned to march and stand, to drill, to salute, to suffer hazing. We learned military etiquette! We were subject to the wishes and direction of upper classmen, those who had arrived to fill the class before us. This was military orientation for the Class of 41B—the second class to come out of Tulsa in 1940 on its way to graduation in a fateful year.

It was the happiest year of my life. I was 22 years old. I had 130 flying hours in the records. I was where I wanted to be, learning what I wanted to know, becoming what I wanted to be, acquiring a skill from the best there were to teach it, training with the best, flying with the best. My primary purpose in life had been to fly. I was flying.

I was also driving a new ragtop. As soon as the San Antonio auto dealers were satisfied that a cadet would be making it through basic, meaning he could meet the $28 per month car payments, the showrooms welcomed him. I came out with a black Ford convertible topped by white canvas and immediately had the wheels painted red to complement my white sidewall tires. My spirits were really flying now. This was freedom!

From Randolph we transferred across town to Kelly Field for Advanced Pilot Training.

My first taste of jeopardy in Advance Training may not have supplied me with any expertise in scrambling through combat jams, but it did give a clue to my resourcefulness.

Of necessity, a pilot is a quick thinker, in peace or war, in clouds or clear air, night or day. It was now time in the training schedule to prove I was at home in the sky whatever the conditions. It was the occasion for my first night cross-country flight.

My training cohorts at Kelly Field and I already had flown daylight cross-country. In Texas cadets can fly a technical cross-country and never leave the state. And we had already flown point-to-point at night, starting at Kelly, heading toward predetermined destinations and returning to Kelly.

We were training four students to an instructor on an AT-6, capable of 160 to 170 miles an hour, a big single-engine plane with a big engine and a crew of one—the pilot. The cockpit was a tandem two-seater with one seat reserved for a flight instructor when he chose to fly with any of his student pilots. Usually the student flew by himself.

Lieutenant Davis, our regular flight instructor, had been personally responsible throughout our Advance Flight Training for all aspects of our flight experience. We each racked up 75 hours in the air under his guidance. He held ground training lectures with us. He talked privately with each of us. From time to time, he flew with each of us individually. He flew with the four of us in formation, in trail flying, in cross-country. He pushed for our success. He had confidence in us. As he groomed us for careers in the air his single, constant fear was that one of us eagerly flying too close behind would chew up his tail with a propeller.

He scheduled our first night cross-country and designated the check points outside the San Antonio area—southwest to Eagle Pass on the Rio Grande, up to Fredericksburg, over to Austin, south to New Brownsville and back into San Antonio.

Night fell. The four of us flew out of Kelly at five minute intervals, Lieutenant Davis flying with one of the other students. As each pilot passed over the designated checkpoints that the routing prescribed, he was to call in to the instructor something like "Flight number 13 turning over Eagle Pass en route Fredericksburg" and adjust his heading for the new course.

And five minutes following, the next pilot would call in "… turning over Eagle Pass en route Fredericksburg." If everyone was on schedule, each pilot would report in five minutes after the previous pilot as the checkpoints were crossed.

I took off last in line from San Antonio into a very dark sky. In short order I knew I was lost somewhere between San Antonio and Eagle Pass—my running lights were the only lights I saw. Running lights protect planes in flight from hitting each other; other than that they are worthless. Now I was seeing my worthless lights and absolutely no others in the sky.

Without distance measuring equipment (DME), without radio VHF, without the running lights of the other planes ahead of me, with only radio beacons and dead reckoning—heading, time and distance determining location—I was alone, and lost. I was supposed to be heading for the minimal lights of Eagle Pass and the river but it seemed that I wasn't.

And I was tense and impatient, a common curse of new pilots flying dead reckoning, impatient to see the lights of their destinations. I had made a flight correction but my gut feeling was that I was not heading toward Eagle Pass. My confidence sagged and I made another correction, unnecessarily. And maybe another. None of them seemed to be doing the job. I was lost. Had I held the original course long enough, I probably would have been right in line.

Feeding my disorientation was the fear that I would cross the Rio Grande into Mexico. Flying in a foreign country's air space had consequences I didn't want to have hanging on me.

Behind me I could still see the glow of the lights of San Antonio serving as a tempting salvation. So tempting they were that I made a 180 degree turn and headed back to that familiar brightness. I climbed to an altitude of 10,000 feet, 4,000 feet higher than our assigned altitude for the night flying experience and quite safe from other traffic. I was really alone now, above the student pilots. Predating the installation of radar, I was beyond any airport control, flying around over San Antonio in a world that was unaware of my deviousness.

I calculated where my flight instructor was and where I was supposed to be in relation to him in time and space. In less than an hour the pilots would start calling in. When the reports began I waited my turn through five-minute intervals and called in—"Henebry over Eagle Pass, turning 42 degrees . . ." And again, "Henebry over Fredericksburg turning 81 degrees on course Austin . . ." "Henebry over Austin . . ."

And all the while I was circling San Antonio at 10,000 feet—the only pilot in that rare air—waiting for the three planes, one of them carrying our instructor, to complete their first three-hour night cross-country test and return for Kelly Field landings at five minute intervals underneath my circling plane.

After the Austin call-ins I calculated I had 35 more minutes until the AT-6s started coming in. I again waited my turn, coolly called in, entered the traffic pattern, descended and landed, finally exiting my plane to receive the congratulations due pilots who successfully complete their first night cross-country flying.

I was a flying cadet as I circled over San Antonio. I have since moved up through the ranks of the military and of life and have never publicly confessed that transgression. I confess now. It's too late to wash out of Advanced Training, of the military or of life.

How different a year and some months later, another first night flight. This one with more at stake, flying a warship without any running lights or landing lights through unknown turbulent skies, crossing a 13,000 foot mountain range at midnight to a war-battered airstrip outside an unlit jungle town. The initial fear. The ultimate satisfaction in adding this adventure to a growing list of new experiences. How soon we accustomed ourselves to the tricks of night flying.

Finally on March 14, 1941, we were singing out loud the classic "I wanted wings; now I got the goddamn things." That day, the last of my flying school days, I was graduated with 207 flying hours, those silver wings and a second lieutenant's gold bars. We were the second of four crops of pilots turned out by Kelly in 1941. A stable of newly-trained pilots was all the U.S. military could boast of in the spring of 1941. Material was short and airplanes were old—the B-25 had not yet been delivered and what the Army Air Corps possessed were the same planes that had come through the previous war.

Spring, 1941: I had less than a year of peace left in my youth.

John Henebry received his Silver Wings and Second Lieutenant promotion in March, 1941

Fate

"WHAT type of planes do you want to fly and where do you want to fly them?" After months of training every cadet pretty much knew what adventurous road he intended to follow.

The pre-war Army Air Corps flying school had a policy of offering its graduating cadets a range of choices as they closed in on their wings and bars: Do you want to pilot a transport, a fighter, a bomber, a reconnaissance plane? Do you want duty Stateside or overseas? The inherent promise was the Army would, if it could, fill the graduates' desires.

After considerable discussion with my classmate and good friend, Jack Brown, buoying each other's frontiersman spirit, we decided to opt for the Philippines. We had heard reports about friendly people, tropical atmosphere, ideal flying conditions, superb facilities, top notch airports and exotic destinations beyond the base. Such a romantic outlook we had.

I was already somewhat familiar with the territory because of the friends I had made previously among the Filipino student population at Notre Dame. Jack and I both felt the exotic attraction.

With that decision finalized, late one afternoon we each filled out the school's questionnaires probing our intentions and took them down to our flight line office to cast our lot.

On the way back to our barracks we stopped by the Officers Club for a beer. The Officers Club was a perk offered to graduating cadets as they approached their final days of training and we often took full advantage.

Sitting at the bar overhearing us preview our destinies was an old Army Air Corps captain—old to us being an officer probably in his early forties and of rank exalted to those of us not yet sporting bars.

The captain asked if we knew what our assignments were to be after our graduation. We said "no decisions yet" but that we had signed up for the Philippines. He thought the choice was quite unusual for a kid from the Midwest and asked why I had selected that part of the world. We confessed that we had heard such adventuresome tales about the duty there and looked forward to the experience.

His overseas assignments had been vast, had included our choice and he agreed that the Philippines had been pleasant duty. But, he warned, if we were looking for flying, that station was really not the place to be. Everything was in short supply except mosquitos and nets. The Army Air Corps there had only a few operating airplanes, outdated at that, with replacement parts and mechanics always in short supply. Keeping the planes in commission was a continual problem. Flight activity was at a minimum. He painted a very gloomy picture and suggested we stay in the States.

As a result of this chance meeting with the "old timer" Jack and I rethought our earlier decision. We reluctantly reached the conclusion that if we wanted to get the most flying experience and flying time possible, we needed to forget foreign adventures.

The next morning we went down to the flight line at Kelly Field where our records were kept. We asked the sergeant who handled the administrative details if the materials including our assignment questionnaires had arrived and had our requests for assignment been noted. "Yes," he said, "they had." When we expressed our desire to change our preference, "a little late," he responded. He already had typed up the complete lists for assignment. He looked for our names through the 200-plus cadets on the four hand-typed pages of neatly organized officers and destinations and found that both our first requests for assignment, the Philippines, had been honored. In fact, true to the Army's promise, everyone who had requested the Philippines was on that list—some 25 graduating cadets.

The sergeant balked. "To remove our names," he tried to explain, "would cause a lot of trouble," the primary problem we surmised being his having to reorganize and manually type the modified lists anew. We became aware that he was not saying it would be absolutely impossible to retype the lists all over again, but . . .

Thus encouraged, we hung around the office chumming and trying to persuade a non-com in control of our future careers to put that first piece of paper into the typewriter.

After some time the sergeant realized how serious we were. He agreed to retype the lists with our names moved to the Stateside duty list. So it was my first assignment placed me in Virginia with the Second Squadron of the Twenty-second Group, an old time Army Air Corps unit at an old time Army base called Langley Field.

Later events made this a momentous change of direction. Every cadet who had requested and been granted the Philippine assignment eventually was sent for duty at Clark Field north of Manila. Every classmate sent to Clark Field was there when the Japanese staged their vicious follow-up attack December 8, 1941.

Their fate is history. Ten thousand American troops trapped by the invading Japanese. Seven hundred Americans beaten to death, shot or beheaded in a forced 70 mile march to prison camp—the Bataan Death March. Six thousand more died of starvation and disease in camp.

What happened individually to each of them I do not know. One classmate, my friend Herb Glover, had become an infantry officer in charge of a platoon at Clark Field. He survived the Japanese invasion of Luzon, escaped the conquest and occupation. He managed to stay alive by skirting the enemy, avoiding capture while snaking his way down through the Philippines, miraculously ending up in Australia's North Queensland, where I met up with him again at Charters Towers. He was now a seasoned warrior. I was then fresh from submarine patrol out of Savannah, Georgia.

Fate. Realizing now the horror of the early Philippine war experiences I avoided by looking for better flying, better equipment and better facilities Stateside, I think the good Lord was tending that bar, looking after me.

So I thank the Army for offering us early Officers Club privileges where we gathered to plot our futures. And I thank that wise and experienced "old" captain for steering us away from a field with second-rate equipment, shamefully unprepared for war. And where would I have been but for the accommodating sergeant who ultimately agreed to move a couple of names around on a couple of sheets of paper?

I would have wound up in the Philippines tragic years before I ultimately arrived in victory as a full colonel. I would have been doomed to the horrible fate of those unfortunate classmates who were looking only for the adventures of flying in the tropical skies of the peaceful Pacific during the summer of 1941.

First Hits

Asea gull prepared me for the shock of Pacific battle.

I had touched down around noon December 7, 1941, at Morrison Field outside West Palm Beach and was shutting down my engines when the line chief reported "The Japanese are bombing Pearl Harbor. The whole Pacific fleet has been bombed to hell." A call to my squadron headquarters advised me to refuel and immediately fly my B-18 back to home base, now Orlando.

Congress had not yet declared war but we knew we were in it and reacted accordingly. Everyone in the military had assumed war for some time, as we followed the Axis expansion activities in Europe and Africa, not knowing when or where the spark would ignite. The Japanese were restless in the Far East. "Something bad's gonna happen," summarized most discussions. In the spring of 1941 FDR had said, "They hate us. Sooner or later they'll come after us." He had already called for the production of 50,000 airplanes a year. On December 2nd, Japanese reconnaissance planes were photographing Clark Field in the Philippines. Pearl Harbor had never been indicated.

I found a quiet and business-like atmosphere when I returned to Orlando. All personnel were leaving phone numbers where they could be reached. Half the numbers were Phil Berger's Bar in downtown Orlando. The remainder were at Dubsdread Country Club. Orlando in 1941 was still a quiet little Florida town of some 30,000 permanent residents with few places to hide. Disney had not yet brought in the crowds.

By December 8, the actual day war was declared, three B-18s, mine among them, were assigned to Hunter Field at Savannah, reporting to the Southeast Anti-Submarine Command Headquarters. The military was quick to put its war pieces in place.

Our patrol orders put 15 or 20 of us out over four to five hundred miles of coastal waters—from Bangor, Maine, to the Straits of Yucatan—for four, five or six hours at a stretch. Rumors of spies on Florida shores and U-boats cruising the Gulf of Mexico made our flights significant. Flying at 2,000 feet without bombs or depth charges, we searched for German submarines in the primary commercial shipping lanes off the eastern shore. The Germans had already been at work attacking and harassing foreign shipping in the Gulf Stream. Sub patrols were also scouting off the west coast and the Australians were covering the Pacific.

We buzzed whatever ships we spotted, flying in close enough to note whatever names we could, record and report what we noted.

Enemy submarines were difficult to detect. They seldom surfaced during the daylight hours when we maneuvered. Our only chance would have been subs running with periscopes up preparing for a daylight attack or crash diving in emergency moves, attempting to hide. Either action would have been an oddity during sun up. Safe in those pre-sonar and pre-radar times, enemy subs normally surfaced only at night and every night to run their diesel engines and recharge their batteries long after we had returned to base.

In my first six months of war flying sub patrol, I never saw a sub nor a periscope. Our greatest service to the security of the shipping lanes was to keep enemy submarines suppressed below periscope depth where they were unable to fire torpedoes. The constant presence of B-18 sub patrollers kept the enemy at that non-threatening level, or spurred them into crash diving to safety.

We would see and report the results of war work—damaged military and commercial ships, oil slicks indicating sunken ships and recovery ships and crews heading toward sea disasters to assist in rescue. We would confirm previous reports of German torpedo attacks against lone and very vulnerable Allied shipping vessels supplying military campaigns. The Germans were sinking a lot of ships at that time.

Later in the war, ships traveled in 80 to 100 ship convoys escorted by warships, observation and barrage balloons, and patrol planes. But in these first months of the war, the Atlantic Ocean around North America was pretty much empty space.

Sammy was my co-pilot in that B-18 with its tight plexi-glassed turret in the nose housing a 30-caliber machine gun. Flying along at 500 feet, at about 145 to 155 miles per hour, we pulled up to get in position to buzz a sighted freighter. We wanted to check out its name and nationality when WOW, we felt the thud and heard the air rush of a hit.

Sammy jumped up out of the co-pilot's seat and said, "Let's get the hell out of here. They're firing at us!"

I didn't think that ship had fired but I knew something had hit us and needed to find out what. Sammy volunteered to go down into the nose to check the situation. When he opened up the door on the floor behind the co-pilot's seat stuff flew all through the airplane—bird stuff—feathers and innards. We obviously had hit a sea gull.

February 1942, my first WWII combat damage. On the other side of the world the Japanese were preparing for their first attack on Australia.

"Close the damn door. We gotta stop that rush of air through the turret," was my first combat order.

The turret was demolished. Floating feathers filling the cockpit forced us back to base at Hunter Field. Once we had landed, we had to face our crew chief who surveyed the damage and the mess inside his plane and wondered out loud, "What in god's name have you guys been up to?" It was he who would have to replace the turret and scrub down the plane's interior. "There's not even enough left of the bird to mount," was his lament.

That old pre–World War II B-18 Douglas twin-engine all-metal bomber we flew was serving its last official time in the air. When it was introduced in the 1930s, it was the most advanced bomber for its time.

I was moving along too, serving my last official days as a sub patroller in the Thirty-Ninth Squadron/Thirteenth Group—certainly not my fantasized aviation career. The sea gull contact had been my only excitement in this early stage of the war. The action obviously was elsewhere. We were all looking for something else to do.

In June of 1942 the call came to the anti-sub patrols for overseas combat volunteers. Needed were six pilots who would choose crews of five each. The job description: aviators who could fly, shoot down enemy planes, sink enemy ships, put bombs on a target.

I lined up Lieutenant Lee "Pop" Hicks, an eager co-pilot; top turret gunner Sergeant Dietz, a bus driver from New Jersey; a top navigator Lieutenant Dave McComber from Bowdoin College in Brunswick, Maine, a man who looked like his feet wouldn't track, studious, funny, but able to follow his pilot knowing exactly where the plane was at all times, knowing the speed, knowing the altitude, the direction, able always to pinpoint location; Lieutenant R. R. "Railroad" Martin as bombardier, a necessary function when bombs were dropped from eight to eleven thousand feet with the aid of the Norden bombsight; and Sergeant Moore, a radio operator/lower turret gunner. A crew on its way to war. We stayed together for quite some time after we joined the battle.

Getting an effective air crew together was serious business. A pilot looked for people who wanted to fly with him, men who wanted to be in combat. These were to be his guys, assigned to his leadership. The pilot was commander of the aircraft, responsible for these men. As their pilot, their lives were in my hands. They depended on my being good. My primary goal was to keep us alive by keeping myself alive. In doing that I would avoid hurting myself and I wouldn't hurt my men. Get through the battle. Get them through. In the battles to come, I did lose a plane but I never lost a man.

I went to the Pacific as a new silver-barred first lieutenant with a $50 pay raise, now at $255 per month, assigned to the undermanned, underequipped, undertrained, underfed Third Attack Group operating out of Charters Towers in Queensland, northeastern Australia. The Third, with a 23-year history of bombardment, became known before this war was won for its low altitude, hedge-hopping attacks, "sweeping into their targets under cover of a grass-cutting hail of machine gun fire and dropping delayed fuse bombs with deadly precision" (General Kenney's appraisal). The Third also came out of the war with the lowest combat casualty record in the Fifth Air Force. I joined the war with two solid years of flying experience in some of the latest equipment then being produced. Since my graduation I had flown B-18s, PT-17s, A-29s and the newly designed B-25s. Whatever experience I had incorporated would help preserve me in the combat to come.

We laid over for three weeks at Hamilton Field near San Francisco waiting transport to Australia, raising hell with the money we all had cleared selling our cars back east.

Pop Hicks had picked up a bride in Chicago. When he discovered his Pacific destination, he made arrangements to bring his girl and her parents to the Palmer House on State Street, downtown Chicago, married her there and smuggled her onto the troop train to honeymoon in San Francisco.

George "Spike" Thomas, another of the sub patrol pilots, had a brother, a graduate of the Military Academy, on Stateside duty with the Navy. While Spike was making efforts in vain to contact his mother or his brother with the news of his overseas assignment, she had found out and was on her way to San Francisco, waiting as a surprise at the ramp when the ferry boat took us across the bay from Oakland. It was a joyous moment and she joined our merry band in our San Francisco celebrations. Six months later Spike was dead, lost in thick weather returning from New Guinea to his base at Charters Towers.

Six of our anti-sub B-25 crews, headed by pilots Oscar Wertz, Tommy Cline, Lieutenants Simmons and Raymond Peterson, Spike and me—36 of us from the Thirteenth Group out of Savannah—joined thousands of GIs aboard the former Mt. Vernon, a 24,000 ton troop transport ship out of San Francisco en route to Australia, supposedly with top secret orders that we all knew.

Of these original six pilots, this rootin', tootin', shoot'em-up gang from the eastern shore, now bonded together by a journey and a mission never imagined in our days of training, only Tommy Cline and I came home alive from that Pacific war. Cline, alive still and a retired lieutenant colonel in Kentucky, flew his required 50 missions and rotated out of the theater.

Our troop ship traveled alone, no convoys yet in the early days of the war. We zig-zagged down the Pacific, avoiding detection and danger. Down the globe we went, past Tahiti. Down we went.

After 21 days non-stop the ship put in at Wellington, New Zealand. There, the captain checked the activity of Japanese submarines. We then moved over to Auckland, checking again. Finally, the captain was cleared to continue west across the Tasman Sea to Sydney, Australia.

Tommy Cline and John Henebry in 1943 in New Guinea

We again waited for our troop train north to Brisbane. Then after another couple-days wait another train on a narrow gauge railroad took us north past 20-foot high anthills and desert to Townsville on the north coast of Queensland. This was turn-of-the-century transit, toilet facilities in the train cars, but no food. At all the various stops along the route the ladies of the town met us with sandwiches, coffee and tea. We would jump off, eat a quick snack and continue on.

Trucks met us at Townsville and carried us 75 miles inland to the old gold mining and cattle breeding town of Charters Towers. We crossed over into a replay of the American wild west of the nineteenth century.

MacArthur had arrived three months previous to find an armed force of only 32,000 Allied troops, a destroyed navy and less than 100 airplanes. "God have mercy on us," was his reaction.

The Fifth Air Force's huge battlefield

The Australians had built a 6,000-foot black-top runway on the edge of Charters Towers, preparing for total war. It was a beginning. MacArthur believed that "the nation that does not command the air will face deadly odds. Armies and navies to operate successfully must have air cover." Supply was the key to victory according to this master strategist and we airmen would protect the life lines from an envisioned string of bomber bases stretching from New Guinea to Manila.

Mid-1942, Third Attack Group Officers Club at Charters Towers:
Col. Jim Davies (standing top row with mug in right hand), Col. Paul "Pappy" Gunn
(sitting second row from bottom center with cast on his right hand). On Pappy's left is
Lt. Col. Bob Strickland who followed Davies as Third Attack Group Commanding Officer.

At Charters Towers we joined the three remaining squadrons of our newly assigned Third Attack Group waiting for bases to be built in New Guinea. The Eighty-Ninth Squadron, first with a full complement of airplanes, some of them reportedly conned from the Dutch air force in Melbourne with false orders, had already hopped across the Coral Sea to an airdrome three miles out of Port Moresby on the south coast of New Guinea. There the men were engaging the Japanese, who were approaching across the Owen Stanley Range intent on establishing this forward base for another invasion attempt on Australia. The

Eighty-Ninth was the first American unit to fly combat against the Japanese out of New Guinea airstrips.

It was August—the middle of tropical winter. Seasons were the reverse of what I had been accustomed to and 50 degrees hotter, 25 inches wetter with mosquitos biting year round. Our six crews, now assigned to the Ninetieth Squadron, were told where to pitch our four-man squad tents. We established our new homes from issued canvas, tent poles, and mosquito nets, and accustomed ourselves to the tented mess hall and Australian bully beef.

Pilots arriving at Charters Towers initially set up with four-man squad tents

Several days were devoted to "orientation" before we reported to the flight line. The timing had been exquisite: we left Barksdale in June, arrived in July, were ready for "go" in August. But the squadron was seriously short of planes as was the whole Pacific air force. As critical as was the Allied situation in this theater, Washington theory gave the first priority to Europe. We were to fight the Japanese the best we could with what we had. It was an operational plan agreed upon December 22 by FDR and Churchill. The Germans were the priority enemy.

The Japanese—now just 31 miles from Port Moresby and fanning out all over this strategic island—were a very significant enemy, more important than Washington held them. Theirs was not a third rate air force. They had, after all, aggressively attacked us and their air capabilities remained noticeably superior. They dominated the skies over Port Moresby. Their bombers could operate above our intercepting planes, bombing us at will. Their nimble Mitsubishi Zeros were superior to our P-40 Warhawks—fast, light, sensitive, more maneuverable with powerful engines and better high altitude capabilities. The Zero was a superb and deadly fighter plane.

But it provided its pilots neither protective armor nor self-sealing fuel tanks. Their armament, too, wasn't the four-to-six fifty-caliber machine guns our P-40s used. Twenty-seven calibers was their best. They did carry heavy 20 millimeter guns.

Their airmen were experienced fighters, excellent gunners and practiced pilots, their units having been under meticulous combat training since 1931 when Japan began its serious and successful expansion policy. The current pilots were professional warriors, dedicated to their country with skills sharpened on Chinese pilots and their supporters since the launch of that war in 1937. They were as good as, if not better, than any group of Western pilots we had in the air at that time.

This was an enemy that held death more honorable than capture with pilots who didn't wear parachutes.

What we had were some, not enough, obsolete P-39s, P-40s, a few antiquated A-24 dive bombers and old A-20 light bombers, the only aircraft designed specifically for attack combat. This was the Army's original contribution to the Australian theater. A few B-25s from the Dutch sweetened the pot. Our squadron had some equipment; other squadrons had nothing. Parts were in short supply. Wrecked planes were scavenged to repair damaged aircraft. The Third was in a Herculean struggle to put a second outfit into combat readiness and to maintain it.

Expanding and re-equipping with personnel and material, airplanes, spare parts, fuel, while a war rages is a confusing endeavor. Morale was low. It wasn't a match. The Japanese Zeros were beating us.

More pilots than planes were hanging around Charters Towers. But soon my crew and I were assigned to a B-25 for orientation and post-inspection testing flights in the area. We relished the chance to get back into the air. Hicks, Martin, McComber, Deitz, Moore and I added a newly assigned crew chief, Sergeant Al Deemie, to our team. He kept our airplane in top mechanical condition, guns loaded, bombs in the correct configuration. Our plane was his plane and he was part of our tight little group.

Now we primarily flew our B-25 over the Australian countryside and while most flights were quite uneventful, one approach and landing tested our skills. Three red lights were indicating the two main landing gears and the nose wheel were not locking down. Trying everything, including the emergency cranking system, I found nothing worked. The landing gear control was in the down position, the gears were up, the lights stayed red and the warning horn was making a hell of a racket.

All procedures seemingly exhausted, the Ninetieth Squadron commander now in the control tower advised us to make our choice—bail out or belly land that precious plane on the runway.

I made my decision and canvassed the crew, which included on that flight our crew chief. I was sticking; they could bail out or stay with me and the plane. I had overcome a similar situation a few months earlier with a B-25 at Westover Field without a problem. Then, the nose and the left gear had come down. The right landing gear had stayed up. The emergency cable crank would not budge. Two greens and a red. We had flown over Westover for a couple of hours, burning excess gasoline, making us very light and less flammable. In those couple of hours maneuvering in the air we had tried to spring the locked wheel loose. Finally, we were instructed to bring it in on a wide grassy area, parallel to the runway. The B-25 had stayed straight and level until the wing lost its lift throwing us into a 90 degree loop on grass. A fine landing. No crew damage. Minimal plane damage.

I reminded this crew of the success of that landing. I knew, due to its low belly configuration, this B-25 could make an even better landing with all wheels-up.

The crew elected to stay with the plane with three lights in the red and warning horns blasting. A short, rough landing indeed. How true the aviation adage: Flying is the second greatest thrill known to man. Landing is the first.

Our line chief, Master Sergeant Foreman, supervised the inevitable repair. The crew jacked the B-25 where it stopped on the runway, cranked the gears down and towed it to the squadron repair area to attend to the bent blades of both propellers and the damaged underbelly. In less than a month it was flying combat.

Extensive B-25 time before going into actual battle was a plus here with that landing and later, eventually saving my life.

Now in the saddle, to get into the fight we flew from Charters Towers across the Coral Sea to Port Moresby. We flew combat out of its nearby airstrip and slept in tents. The lack of available airfields in New Guinea forced this constant shuttling. When we had spent all our bombs and ammunition and the planes were ready for refurbishing and inspection we rotated back to Charters Towers, loaded up again and returned to Port Moresby.

Out of Charters Towers, we prayed for ceiling and visibility unlimited (CAVU) weather and a clear sighting of the Osprey Reef with its halo of pale pink waters in the deep blue sea. The reef's major beauty from eight-to-ten thousand feet is the comfort it gives, confirming you are halfway to Port Moresby and on course. The war imposed radio silence, reducing us to flying dead reckoning, and the Osprey Reef was the only navigational aid available. These were Navigator Dave McComber's first over-water flights of any appreciable distance. My co-pilot, Pop Hicks, and I, flying manual without automatic pilot equipment, would hit Osprey and Port Moresby right on the nose and cheer. The whole operation eventually became a hands-on piece of cake.

Finally in October, after a couple of trips south to Brisbane to pick up some converted B-25s with bomb sights removed and additional fifty-caliber machine guns installed, orders to move north permanently 600 miles across the Sea to Papua New Guinea came for me, my crew and a couple other of our squadron's B-25 crews. The destination was the newly built Seven-Mile/Jackson Field and combat orientation. All Port Moresby airfields were named for their distance from that city, (i.e. Three-Mile where the Eighty-Ninth Squadron was based, Seven-Mile, eventually Eleven-Mile and Seventeen-Mile where our Ninetieth Squadron ultimately was based). Our engineers were hacking airstrips out of the jungle as fast as our plane inventory increased. We left the Eighth behind in Australia to become our airplane M&R stop for engine changes and heavy maintenance.

We landed at Seven-Mile, reported to base operations, let the "Follow Me" Jeep lead us to the dispersal area and stood by our planes for further instruction.

Japanese low level strafing attacks in this area seemed everywhere. The enemy's air superiority was yet to be effectively challenged with our defense remaining dangerously short of fighter aircraft.

The Japanese attacked by air and were approaching by land. Inconceivably, their troops had surged over the Owen Stanley Mountain range through the 7,600-foot high Kokoda Pass. Skilled at jungle warfare, they successfully battled the dense tropical rainforest's hot days and frigid nights, through swamps and bogs and mud and dead foliage and restrictive vines, over rocks and slopes, plagued by insects, disease and starvation. They actually were threatening Port Moresby and its surrounding airfields.

Fortunately, the Australians, with some help from the Yank ground forces and the A-20s of the established Eighty-Ninth Squadron, pretending they owned the skies, held them at Kokoda and eventually turned back the advance within 25 miles of the Port Moresby airstrips. General George Kenney masterminded the troop movements for the Allied support and the success with which he used his air force helped to instill in the mind of MacArthur a confidence in air power as the new way to fight a war. After tremendous loss of life, the Japanese ground advancement ended January 2, 1943, in one of Japan's early tragic and humiliating defeats.

General Kenney standing before a Grim Reapers logo

The combined action brought the comments of George C. Marshall, then Army Chief of Staff. "Air forces, by repeatedly attacking the enemy ground forces and installations and by destroying his convoys made possible the success of ground operations . . . The courage, spirit and devotion to duty of all elements of the command made possible the complete victory attained."

It was perfectly clear that Port Moresby had nothing to offer but location. The Japanese strategy targeted it as the center of a proposed blockade or possible invasion of northern Australia.

Port Moresby boasted no industry nor exports worth fighting for. It was a native village with a small population at the end of nowhere served by missionaries, a couple of minor hotels, a couple of government buildings, some newly established Allied airfields and a harbor—and a full thriving population of mosquitos. Native markets instead of stores offered coconuts, roots, rice, fish, yams, some limited fruit and betel-nut—none of which appealed to the Australians or Yanks. And beer—which did. Even with a million kina in your khakis you were poor in Port Moresby.

By the late summer of 1942 our B-25s were conducting serious day and night reconnaissance flights out of Port Moresby, carrying ammunition to protect ourselves and bomb loads to take advantage of targets of opportunity. The Japanese were running in supplies to the north coast by submarine and destroyers. Our routes took us over the Owen Stanley Range and the Solomon Sea to the south coast of New Britain. Or we moved up the north coast of New Guinea to Salamaua and Lae in the Huon Gulf, back to the Buna/Gona area, south across the Owen Stanley Range following the Kokoda Trail, returning to Port Moresby.

Port Moresby, New Guinea

On one such mission, sea gull experience under my belt, we were making our turn in the Huon Gulf, ready to head back toward base when I saw my first Japanese fighter.

Surprisingly he was alone—the Japanese normally didn't venture out into contested air by themselves. He might have been on a reconnaissance flight, too. Or on patrol, protecting his territory. Or he might have been sent to alert our northern coast enemy targets—Salamaua or Lae. Mid-1942 the Japanese didn't yet have a radar warning system.

Whatever his purposes, he and his lone Zero were in the air with us at eight to ten thousand feet. He intercepted us without firing, made a pass and then flew along for several minutes at our altitude, hanging to the left out of range of our guns. I asked myself, "Why the hell is that guy doing that?" He was taking a good look at our B-25, probably as new to him as his Zero was to me.

B-25 pilots were advised that a successful defensive move when opposed by faster enemy fighters was to increase speed by putting the airplane in a slight descent, accelerating power. Since a B-25 can never outrun a Zero, picking up speed in a descent was our only sensible maneuver.

Once we started that descent, the Zero decided to make a pass, putting himself within range of our turret guns—two fifty-calibers in each of the top and lower turrets. Deitz shot him down. On one of our first combat missions in the Pacific theater of war we now had our first Zero sighting, our first kill. It gave us confidence that whenever we met this enemy we could coolly defend ourselves.

We were proud to bring this plane back untouched, no feathers, no guts, no bullet holes.

5
New Guinea

THE days following the Pearl Harbor attack teemed with speculation. On the "date which will live in infamy" a flurry of facts and fictions erupted among the military and civilian populations. "What did these Japanese want?" was our basic question.

What became increasingly obvious was that what "they" wanted were secure trade routes to protect the critical delivery of food, materials and energy to their home islands. Possession of the Philippines and southeast Asia seemed vital.

An even more essential desire was the removal of the "white devils"—the Americans, British, French and Dutch—from the Japanese-designed Greater East Asia Co-Prosperity Sphere, freeing the Japanese, this self-acclaimed superior race, to deal on their terms with the Chinese and the many other nationalities and cultures in these thousands of square miles of land and sea. Their ambitions for control were total and unhampered by any sense of humanity toward those they were conquering. They would fight to the death for that control.

Ultimately it was the militarists in Japan who convinced their government they could throw out these unwanted influences in the orient and establish Japanese dominance over east Asian destiny. These were military forces who had never experienced defeat through years of battling inferior forces and, along with the whole of the Japanese population, had become intoxicated with success. Their influence on government policy was pervasive.

On that infamous December day Japan had some 75 million people on its four principal home islands—Honshu, Hokkaido, Shikoku and Kyushu—living on a total land area about the size of California. The mountainous terrain provided too little tillable space to grow too little food for this throbbing population.

Map from September 1943 *Fortune* magazine

Additionally, the island group had very limited natural resources. Scarce essential raw materials—lumber, coal, iron ore, oil, tin and tungsten—needed to be imported. Japan was a hollow factory holding restless masses of eager workers waiting for raw materials, for energy to create a product and for food to fill their guts.

To meet those needs, Japan had been seeking and taking for years. It took Manchuria from China, its first step to an Asian empire, killing and ravaging the conquered. It invaded, brutalized and enslaved Korea and Formosa. One after another north Pacific islands suffered untold indignities. Japan expanded its lifelines bringing in oil from Celebes, Borneo, Indonesia and the Philippines. New Guinea, with a focus on Port Moresby, a major mass of land in position to protect the surrounding seas and islands, was a temptation to these invaders. New Guinea, as a stepping stone to Australia, would be a major stronghold. Australia, with its land mass three quarters the size of the U.S. and its eight to ten million people, would be a fitting goal. If Japan couldn't conquer, its warriors would isolate and prevent interference.

Steady conquest and expansion secured an uninterrupted flow of food and materials to the home islands. However, the strategists' ambitions ultimately moved well beyond sources of food and materials. In the name of territorial security now, the Japanese sought to consolidate their position in the triangle of waters bounded by Japan, Sumatra, and the Solomon Islands. The perimeter blocked off Australia.

Their ambitions, however, were to bring them not the protected waters they craved, but oceans of trouble.

The Japanese strategists misread the territory. They reasoned that if the French were down the drain, perhaps the Dutch were too. The British and Australians in 1941 seemed busily engaged in other war zones. The Americans didn't want any part of war. They anticipated not much interference from any of the white devils. This thinking was close enough to reality to provide the basis for action.

Following their early conquests they broadened their sights to French Indochina, Malaya, the Dutch East Indies, and Thailand. They swept through southeast Asia. Then they focused on Pearl Harbor. Pearl Harbor, the fatal target. The Japanese decided to take on Uncle Sam.

The attack on Pearl Harbor was an attempt to neutralize the U.S. Navy in the Pacific long enough to consolidate the Japanese far-eastern conquests and from that position of strength force America to settle or suffer defeat.

The December 7th attack was a hit and run, providing a tremendous tactical victory. The surprise was total. The Japanese had pulled off a classic strike. Hours later the Japanese hit us again—at an undefended Clark Field in the Philippines with some 200 planes, Mitsubishi bombers and Zero fighters. What a load to bite within so short a time. But settle or suffer we would not. We were suddenly in this war, in it to win.

Impressive as they may have been, the attacks were foolish. They accomplished little. With a couple of regiments as follow-up to the initial strikes, the Japanese could have occupied and controlled prestigious U.S. Pacific territory. True, holding possession would have been difficult because of the extended reach, but for a moment in time Japan might have possessed Oahu and delayed by a couple of years the U.S. ability to strike back, might have delayed their ultimate defeat by a couple of years.

Prior American faults and mistakes contributed to the initial military successes over the U.S. but along with our weaknesses were an industrial strength and potential as well as an attitude in the American people totally misjudged by those in Japan calling the military shots. Americans originally may not have wanted any part of this war, but Pearl Harbor forced an acceptance that became a craving for victory and vengeance. President Roosevelt's overriding goal was to win—no more enemy gains beyond Rabaul. By the time I actually was fighting the Japanese I never had a thought of our losing this war. I was fully committed to the war and its dangers.

Immediately, the December 7 tactical miracle became a strategic blunder of disastrous proportions not only for the attackers but to their Axis allies. The "sleeping giant" awoke and in a few tumultuous hours Japan accomplished what the British had been pressing for years. The "arsenal of democracy" at last was mad enough to go to war, taking on not only the attacking Japanese but the Axis powers as well.

Early intelligence available at my level was pure speculation. I was a mere second lieutenant concerned primarily with German naval infiltration.

By December 8, 1941 Asia and the Pacific Ocean had become more significant. Information continued sparse, coming to us in the lower ranks of the military through the same sources used by the general public—newspapers, magazines, radio. The events of the day stimulated a great deal of discussion and unrest. Among the pilots with whom I served the talk eventually included the possibility of future assignments not in Europe but in combat with an uncharted enemy in uncharted territory.

Unfamiliar place names began popping up in conversations. These newly important names belonged to spots in the vast Pacific. Yes, we could position the Hawaiian Islands, Japan, China, the Philippines, Hong Kong and Australia on the globe but new points—Guam, Wake Island, the Marshalls, the Gilberts, the Java Sea, Bataan, Corregidor, Midway, New Guinea—sent us scurrying to maps, increasingly popular reading material, our major source of geographical statistics and miscellaneous information.

My first combat orders to Australia could lead to New Guinea. Where the hell was New Guinea? Where were the Solomon Islands? Of what use were those thousands of land masses splattered across that ocean? Few of us remembered the lay of those lands from geography lessons. MacArthur arrived from

Corregidor in April 1942 to organize a new battle; I arrived in July to fight it and would look back in later months to admonish the recent arrivals, as ill at ease with the land as I had been: you should have been here when the going was really rough, when we had only a few dozen medium bombers to take to war.

New Guinea, the solid hunk of dark, forbidding terrain poised directly above Australia across the Torres Strait, became the focal point of concern when the Japanese invaded its north coast in March 1942. Even earlier, shortly after the Pearl Harbor invasion, the first serious incursion into the southwest Pacific was the Japanese occupation of Rabaul on New Britain, an island east of New Guinea. Following that, the enemy took control of Guadalcanal in the Solomons to provide a buffer protecting what was to become its major supply base. New Britain, the Solomons, New Guinea at Milne Bay—this voracious enemy was now a mountain mass and a narrow strait away from the Aussies and able to push back her weakened forces toward Port Moresby, a threshold to northern Australia. Before I could begin to adjust my concentration away from German submarines, I was on a ship heading down under.

Then the towering 15,000 foot mountains of New Guinea, the fearsome rain forest jungle vegetation, the marshy coastal plains and the scorching hot and humid tropical climate become important because now I would be piloting a B-25 over those peaks inside undependable, treacherous, tropical, mountainous weather.

At the beginning of the war much of the 300,000 square miles of New Guinea and the majority of other islands in the Pacific war zone were not only undermapped but virtually unexplored. Even George C. Marshall complained, ". . . as far as the Pacific was concerned, if you got a sketch, you were lucky."

This giant island of New Guinea is shaped like a massive turkey running west, taking off from the tip of Cape York Peninsula at the northernmost point of Australia. Its northwest beak rests just short of the equator and its southeast tail dips into the Coral Sea. Like most of the Pacific islands, it is pockmarked with prehistoric volcano eruptions and is covered darkly by creepy jungle. New Guinea had a mighty spine of mountain ranges running 1,500 miles beak to tail and was the second largest island in the world, beat out only by Greenland.

Available prewar maps and aeronautical charts may have been inaccurate, not reflecting land marks and coastal features essential for contact navigation where pilots relate one visible landmark to another en route to a destination. But most treacherous were the errors in placing the mountains and pinpointing their peaks. Some were mislocated by many miles. Particularly in inclement weather these inadequacies often proved to be disastrous—as disastrous as enemy engagements. Consequently, we pilots new to flying uncharted areas learned to give questionably located peaks a wide berth, flying high, wide and safe.

From our sea-level bases on the underside of the island near Port Moresby on the south coast of Papua New Guinea—an Australian protectorate—we regularly climbed the 15,000 feet needed to clear safely the pale blue peaks of the Owen

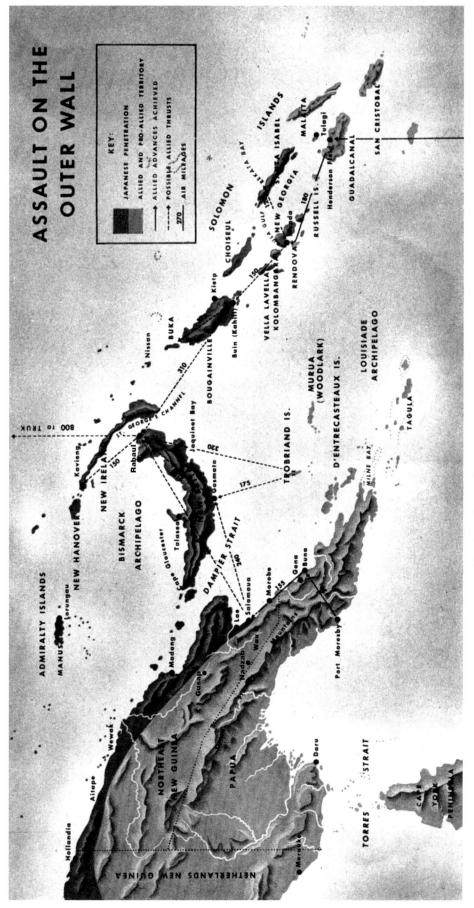

ASSAULT ON THE OUTER WALL

KEY:
Japanese penetration
Allied and pro-Allied territory
Allied advances achieved
Possible Allied thrusts
270 Air mileages

Map from September 1943 *Fortune* magazine

Stanley Range to seek out our well-established Japanese objectives on the north coast. Our B-25s were supercharged to reach those altitudes easily, even fully loaded with fuel, ammunition, bombs and crew. When conditions were CAVU man and machine performed well. It then was a stressless, often wondrous ride.

But since night raids were common and bad weather a norm, CAVU was a rarity and the journey north was often a challenging, treacherous struggle. Returning before the cumulus built up was a survival absolute. At night we flew singly, without lights, in radio silence. The flights were filled with conscientious attention to navigation, to fuel consumption, to speed, to engine operation, to instrument readings, to the mountains and to the enemy.

With such inhospitable conditions, the immediate objective became to get sufficient altitude first before approaching the range. Once for sure across the range we could drop to our assigned 10,000 feet.

That lesson came to me abruptly soon after I arrived, during a daylight flight through cumulus conditions. Picking my way around clouds before reaching an altitude that would carry me safely over the mountains, I looked through a light cloud formation to see on my right an unanticipated mountain peak rising above my plane. Lady Luck or my Lady on the Dome flew with me on that mission. The clouds cleared. The mountain was parallel to me. I was passing by. I said, "No more of this," did a 180-degree turn and from then on climbed to altitude immediately on takeoff and stayed there to avoid an unwelcome face-full of rocks.

I knew New Guinea now.

These were pre-airborne radar times. We had no VHF navigational nor communication aids. We did have radio compasses, but targets, theirs and ours, were blacked out. That left a combination of dead reckoning, the well-proven heading/time/distance technique used by Christopher Columbus to plot a course, and contact, using sights on land or in the water to position the plane. In good weather we could see 60 to 80 miles from 10,000 feet and became quite familiar with the territory, recognizing beaches and coastal marks. But these techniques often failed. We constantly added significant operational losses to our combat losses. More men went down due to inexperienced piloting, bad weather, lack of communication, navigational errors, lack of alternative landing strips, inattention and empty fuel tanks than to actual enemy engagement.

Vital information on our area ultimately came from post-flight debriefings in the operational tents or thatched roof shacks, a pilot's first stop after landing. The squadron intelligence officer met with all mission pilots with forms to fill out, with questions on the mission and to hear the pilots' descriptions of the flights. Did the pilot see the designated target? What did he do about it? What damage did he inflict? Highlights of the accumulated facts, called operational experience, were then available to subsequent missions to assist those pilots in finding and hitting targets and avoiding danger.

Since war is a series of new situations, new experiences and emergencies, besting them depends upon newly available information. Information that can be accumulated through any means, debriefing, code-breaking enemy communications or reconnaissance from 20,000 to 28,000 feet is life-saving.

Inaccurate maps, bad weather, unfamiliar terrain be damned—from the beginning, the one reliable element of our war was our B-25, its airframe and body. And from the beginning, the ground crews who maintained the B-25s were smart, well trained, hard working and dedicated. The aviator's working day began and ended with the ground crew. Mechanical failure was seldom an issue of concern for the airborne man.

In the war zone, all aircraft maintenance and servicing was done in the open. Fuel and oil were transported by ships and trucks, handled under jungle conditions and stored in jerry-rigged containers. Yet I know of no incidents of fuel mishandling or contamination.

There were no hangars. The service crews generally operated off ladders or work platforms in the hard standings back in the bush, hidden from the air by thick foliage. Throughout all the occupied islands of the southwest Pacific and Australia mechanics with imagination rigged shelters over the engines with poles and canvas, pulleys and tree branches. The only exception was the hangar at Eagle Farms in Brisbane where the unceasing B-25 conversions to low level attack strafers were taking place.

The crew chief "owned" the airplane. He and his men were constantly working over the plane, inside and out. It was inspected before and taken apart after each mission. The chief needed to know that at any given minute the plane was ready for battle.

The airframe of the B-25 was very sturdy. It was designed to, and did absorb a lot of damage from enemy ground and air combat. For more than three and a half years, through 219 missions and some 2,000 hours of flying (including 750 hours of combat), our B-25s delivered us home. Fate. Luck. Durable aircraft. Good maintenance.

I have no estimate of how many holes were shot into the airframes of the planes I flew. In spite of the seriousness of some combat situations my crew and I flew through, the planes always remained under control. Through three different belly landings on land and one in the waters off Kiriwina Island, this well-built machine hung together.

The Wright Cyclone 1700 horsepower engines were especially reliable. I lost only two engines, one in a non-combat situation, another received more 20 millimeter shells from a Japanese fighter plane than it could handle.

The dependability of the B-25 and the subsequent aircraft we flew was a major factor in the successes we chalked up in the Pacific war.

While the planes were the best, the early pilots and crews were not afforded the luxury of experience; this massive war was thrust upon us. Many pilots

A B-25 under camouflage in New Guinea where repairs and maintenance were completed

were just out of flying school with little time for transition to the new flying machines coming from the design boards of North American Aviation Company. For many, the most and best training they had was flying their assigned B-25s from America's west coast to Australia and then up to Port Moresby and other South Pacific island bases. Among the first wave to report to Port Moresby, pilot Gordon McCoun had only 22 hours in a B-25 and his co-pilot, Chuck Howe, had only two when they left California and headed west to the war. They survived that Pacific journey and the war to become two of our best soldiers with remarkable combat records.

From left: Estep, Hume, Ken Rosebush, and Gordon McCoun

From left: Chuck Howe, Jones, Burch, and Axt

My pre-combat familiarity was more extensive. Early B-25 experience came through the Accelerated Service Test at Wright-Patterson Air Base during a welcome relief from my sub patrol duties.

Through several months of testing before re-equipping the Third Attack Group, three or four crews on temporary duty from my Orlando outfit flew B-25As at various weights, speeds, attitudes and altitudes; practiced normal and short take-offs and landings; measured temperatures and fuel consumption; flew and landed flaps up and extended; and stalled in all these various configurations. One altitude test brought us up to 30,000 feet, where the air-cooled engines heated up in the thin air. We discovered the B-25's top altitude under control was 21,000 to 22,000 feet, cruising with a load on.

By the time we arrived in Australia, our six crews had ended up with at least 200 hours of concentrated B-25 time, more time than anyone else in our outfit.

Three of those early B-25 pilots from our squadron, Jack Fitzgerald, Oscar Wertz and Tommy Cline, had been called up to Norfolk Navy Air Base. They took three B-25s from our Thirteenth Group in Orlando to spend time in Norfolk practicing short field take-offs. A 500-foot carrier deck outline was painted on the runway and they tested how fast their fuel and bomb-loaded B-25s could get off that painted deck.

The land tests proved so successful that Fitzgerald, his fellow pilots and their planes, carrying sandbags equivalent to the weight of a bomb load, were hoisted by cranes onto the deck of a floating aircraft carrier, the USS *Hornet*, and were taken 100 miles out to sea.

Because a B-25 can become airborne at 57 statute miles per hour, it was expected that under normal circumstances the plane would be able to effortlessly lift off a carrier underway at 20 knots into a 20-knot wind. The expectation was realized. In usual sea conditions it did not take much distance to exceed minimum flying speed. Fitzgerald, flying the lead aircraft, followed by Cline and Wertz, accomplished the first B-25 takeoffs from an aircraft carrier deck.

They flew back to Norfolk. The capability was established. Fitzgerald later reported, "We met a guy there by the name of Doolittle—always observing us. He had a lot of talks with us about how it was to take that B-25 off an aircraft carrier deck. I knew something was cooking. I didn't know whether they were going to have those B-25s on carriers for transport to Europe or North Africa. It sure looked like a ferrying operation." Basis of the surmise: for months the Army Air Corps had been taking P-40s on aircraft carriers across the Atlantic to North Africa, had flown the planes off the carriers and landed them, loaded them and sent them directly into combat. No time wasted.

But Lieutenant Colonel Jimmy Doolittle had other plans for the B-25. He was readying his equipment for his famous morale-boosting April 18, 1942, Tokyo bombing raid off the deck of the USS *Hornet*. He eventually selected his sixteen pilots from the Seventeenth Group at McChord Field in Washington, the first Army Air Corps outfit fully equipped with the Mitchell bomber. Its pilots had accumulated more B-25 experience than our Thirteenth Group in Orlando.

Doolittle's sixteen B-25s were modified for the long-range mission with an additional 225-gallon tank in the upper bomb bay, a 160-gallon tank was added in the crawlway above the wing. The lower turret was removed to accommodate a 60-gallon tank, and 10 five-gallon fuel cans were stowed in the radio operator's compartment with all totaling 1,141 gallons.

Sixteen crews of five men each were selected totaling eighty in all. Due to the sighting of a Japanese surface vessel on the 18th of April 1942 the Doolittle Raiders had to take-off a day early. This in turn made the noble 2,250-mile, thirteen-hour, "30 seconds over Tokyo" an expensive mission. Because of the unplanned early departure and additional miles, all sixteen B-25s were lost on the Raid.

Eleven of the B-25s that bombed Tokyo ran out of fuel and bailed out successfully with their aircraft crashing in China. Four B-25s crash landed off the Chinese coastline, and one B-25 landed in Russia. Of the 80 airmen, eight Raiders were captured by the Japanese from two B-25 crews. Three of the eight were executed, one died in prison, and the four remaining spent the next 40

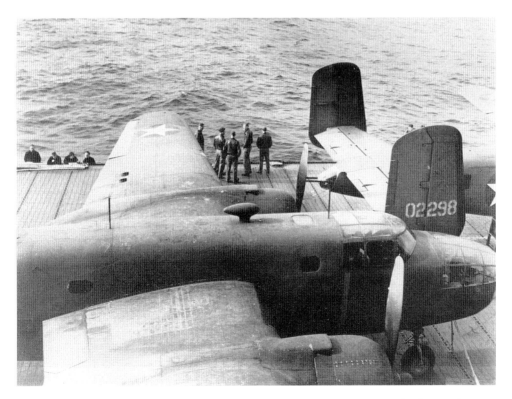

B-25s on board USS *Hornet* en route to Tokyo with "Raiders" huddled in background

The famous medal pinning ceremony on board USS *Hornet*. Doolittle pinned a Japanese medal on one of the 500-lb. bombs to "return" it to Tokyo! Captain of the *Hornet*, Capt. Marc A. Mitscher presents Lt. Col. Doolittle with the medal, with all the famed "Raiders" looking on.

#1 B-25 flies off the USS *Hornet* with Doolittle at the controls, April 18, 1942

months as prisoners-of-war. Two Raiders drowned ditching the B-25s off the Chinese coast and lastly the B-25 crew that landed in Russia was captured and made prisoners-of-war although they escaped and made it back. In all, 70 out of the 80 made it back to safety and were deemed American heroes and many went on to continue to fight in the war.

Doolittle's respect for the B-25 carried over into his postwar career as an oil company executive when he had one of the war horses converted into an elegant corporate transport to test new fuels and lubricants and to carry company officers around the country in luxury.

Ultimately we all reached Tokyo. From the beginning, at every level, we were preparing for that single victorious destination.

The Making of a One-legged Golfer

BEFORE we became low altitude strafers, we often operated three and four hour reconnaissance missions up and down New Guinea's north coast, reconnoitering from several thousand feet looking for targets of opportunity. Nuts or restless, we'd take a crack at anything we could find.

Decisive land victories were not anticipated in the South Pacific. Our battle plan was to conquer troops with deprivation by destroying Japanese air bases on New Guinea and surrounding islands, negating their air superiority and interrupting the enemy's vulnerable supply chain with our growing sea and air power.

Because we had been shooting the hell out of and eventually stopping Japanese transports, destroyers and cruisers supplying their north coast strongholds at Madang, Finschhafen, Lae and Salamaua, the enemy had resorted to using small coastal vessels, mostly diesel-powered launches and barges.

Small and fast, they moved at night, the north New Guinea coastline offering a variety of inlets that provided good hiding terrain. By day the Japanese covered the docked boats with shrubbery and trees. So we became night hunters on search and destroy missions, scouting the 180-some miles of coastal waters between Madang and Wewak for signs of activity. Moonlight hunting was great—searching for the inevitable white phosphorous wakes, getting on the craft before it knew planes were in the air, our machine gun hits being their first awareness of trouble.

During December 1942, intelligence sensed some activity around an insignificant little harbor opposite Manam Island—north of Madang and south of Wewak—Hansa Bay. It was one of a number of coastal shipping staging sites where these boats could slip in during the daytime and be hidden by the intense foliage.

Approaching Hansa Bay we found more than anticipated. Japanese ground fire opened up on us before we had sighted a target, hitting the rear of our fuselage. We could feel the impact and hear the fire rip into us. Checking out the crew, the gunners in the upper and lower rear gun turrets reported one of them bloodied, Sergeant Richard McKinney was hit in the foot.

From left: Epperson, Richard McKinney, Solomon and McKee

I was used to ack-ack by now but I remembered the first time I had experienced it. Pop Hicks, my co-pilot then, and I were flying at 10,000 feet, returning from a recon mission up the north coast of New Guinea when I noticed flashing on the ground. Intelligence had not briefed us regarding anti-aircraft installations in the area and I thought maybe it was trucks with the sun glaring off their windshields or something equally innocent. I turned to Pop and said, "Look at those flashes down there. What the hell is that?" He was equally puzzled until sudden black bursts exploded all around us. We quickly realized the flashes were from anti-aircraft guns they were trying to pop us with. Trying and failing, fortunately their accuracy was off.

Now, damaged and with a wounded man on board, we left the battle at once, heading back to Seventeen-Mile, a two hour flight over the Owen Stanley Range to the Port Moresby area.

The plane ran well. The fuel lines, the electric wiring, the hydraulic lines all were untouched. The hits did not seem to be affecting vital areas. The crew was attending to McKinney, whose left heel had been blown off. A shot of morphine and a tourniquet controlled the pain and the bleeding. McKinney was holding up well.

In emergency situations, and our crippled plane and wounded crewman put us in that category, pilots can break the radio silence kept as a military absolute. So when we were within 100 miles of Seventeen-Mile I called our squadron for a meat wagon reception and was instructed to land at Seven-Mile because of its better emergency facilities and its proximity to a field hospital. The requested ambulance would be waiting there.

Not knowing the extent of the plane's damage, I entered the traffic pattern at Seven-Mile wondering if the landing gear would extend. Landing a plane with a seriously wounded man on board, I wanted to be as gentle as possible and a belly landing would not meet those standards. But thank God we were "three in the green"—all three landing gears extended and locked down.

The medics and one of the crew took McKinney directly to the hospital near Port Moresby and within a few days he was aboard a hospital ship bound for Brisbane, Australia. The doctors were directing all their efforts to avoid gangrene, a major medical threat in the tropics, but lost that battle. Within a couple of weeks McKinney's foot and leg up to his knee had been removed and he was sent home.

All things heal. Hansa Bay, now a tourist attraction in the shadow of an active volcano on Manam Island, is a diver's delight for the abundance of spectacular war wreckage we eventually sent to the bottom of the harbor and the sea life it now supports.

Several years ago during an Eighty-Ninth Squadron reunion in Austin, Texas, a one-legged golfer challenged me to a game. It was McKinney, looking fine, feeling fine and walking well on his prosthetic leg, courtesy of the Veterans Administration, whose doctors and therapists have kept him in the latest prosthetic equipment since they took over his case in Brisbane.

I had pleaded, "Come on Mac, you gotta let me win. I can't go home to tell people that a one-legged guy beat me at golf." He laughed and I won. He may have let me have that victory.

46

Battle of the Bismarck Sea

THE B-25 flew up from Brisbane, Pappy Gunn at the controls. Proudly at the controls. This mechanical genius had just metamorphosed a classic medium altitude bomber into the first low level strafer and skip bomber. Four fifty-caliber machine guns replaced bombardier bomb sights in the nose. He mounted four additional machine guns, two on either side of the fuselage. George Kenney, the impetus behind the conversions, had been the first to fix machine guns on the wing of a plane 20 years earlier. Now, eight pilot-controlled guns fired forward, each supplied with 400 rounds of armor-piercing and tracer ammunition. With two more fifty-caliber machine guns in the rear power turret and four 500-pound bombs in its belly, this B-25 was to be *the* potent attack weapon against enemy ships and ground installations. Military aircraft had come a long way since the WWI days when "fly and look" were the principal war tasks of pilots.

After a year of war in the South Pacific, few remained of the A-20s that had been assigned to the Third Attack Group for the first airmen who arrived in January 1942. The A-20 had been our primary low level strafer, our principal "attack aviation" weapon. No new A-20s from the States were replacing them. Kenney had always preached the value of minimum altitude strafing and decided to replenish the Ninetieth's dwindling stock of A-20s with a converted B-25 capable of duplicating the A-20's potency.

The mid-altitude B-25s we were flying down to Charters Towers from Seven-Mile Field that autumn day were war-weary planes, having flown a series of bombing missions the previous several days. Charters Towers remained our Third Attack Group home base with maintenance facilities capable of putting us back into shape to rotate back to New Guinea and continued missions. There the bomber crews could breathe some fresh air and down some good fresh Australian beer.

In the midst of the maintenance, Pappy and his "Margaret" arrived.

North American B-25 #946 "Margaret" at Eagle Farms, Brisbane, Australia.
The first B-25 converted. Four fifty-caliber machine guns were installed in the nose
and two on each side. Four hundred rounds of ammunition for each gun.

48

The pilots were invited to fly Pappy's newly contrived "engine of death." The plane was to be part of a fruitful theory that this mighty Mitchell bomber could be the center of General George Kenney's attack aviation strategy. Kenney, MacArthur's "Capital A" airman. Kenney, the island's "Number One Balus (airplane) Man." Kenney, commanding all U.S. military aviation and ultimately all Allied aviation including the RAAF (Royal Australian Air Force) and the Dutch—the Netherlands East Indies Air Force. Kenney was launching another formidable instrument of attack. MacArthur's confidence in Kenney stemmed from this ability to improvise and improve, exacting the maximum in fighting qualities from men and equipment.

In "Margaret" the crew was now reduced to three—a pilot, a co-pilot and a top gunner in the back. No navigator needed; no navigational equipment. No bombardier nor bomb sight needed. The pilot assumed those duties and I must say we got pretty good at it. Certainly no more oxygen equipment.

We did a lot of practice firing and low level bombing on range targets set outside of Charters Towers, tearing the hell out of a lot of stuff, having a lot of fun on the deck. Since we had only "Margaret," we would take turns flying her.

"Margaret's" first live hit unfortunately was an Australian cow, grazing peacefully in a pasture. The rancher created some ground turbulence and threatened to sue the U.S. government for damages. We settled out of the diplomatic loop, paying him U.S. dollars pilfered from our officers' mess funds.

We were now attack aviators. We would strafe with forward firing guns used for offense and defense, bomb with high explosive delayed fuse bombs and parafrags from minimum altitude at high speed, fly through fields of fire not knowing who was shooting at us. These would be new experiences a bomber pilot could relish. It was hazardous business. We learned to do it better than anyone.

Flying on the deck personalized the war, made it ours. Flying as low as we could go, we could see details on the trucks and tanks we were shooting up. We could get down on a warship using new tactics that had us hurdling ship masts as we dropped bombs. It made the hunting good. We were the first bomber/strafer outfit in the Air Force. We became Pappy's pet skip bombing boys. Kenney referred to us unofficially as his Attack Group. The name officially stuck.

When I was a student at Notre Dame, trying to direct my career into aviation, I read an article about the Royal Air Force Mosquito and its success in low level strafing of German tanks in the North African desert. I thought then this would be great sport to watch the demolition of your target. A distant dream was now realized.

Our original experience with the B-25 had been medium altitude flight, from eight-to-eleven thousand feet. Our original targets in the Southwest Pacific were shipping—enemy destroyers, light cruisers and submarines running relief supplies in to their troops. From that altitude it was a tough assignment. If you could

PAPPY GUNN'S FUTURE —
South
American
Aviation
Corporation

B-25 PROJECT

BRAD-FOA

spot a Japanese ship, difficult in daylight when ships traveled primarily in bad weather, almost impossible at night, lining up for a bomb run at 10,000 feet was an added, unwanted challenge. Rarely on a clear day would we see a ship at sea. Those we saw could see us also, could see our bombs dropping and could swerve out of danger. Since bombs kept to a predictable course once they left a plane, the ship easily could change direction in the time it took for the bomb to fall.

So the pilots who tried out Pappy's B-25C showed some interest in, and a little enthusiasm for, low level activity.

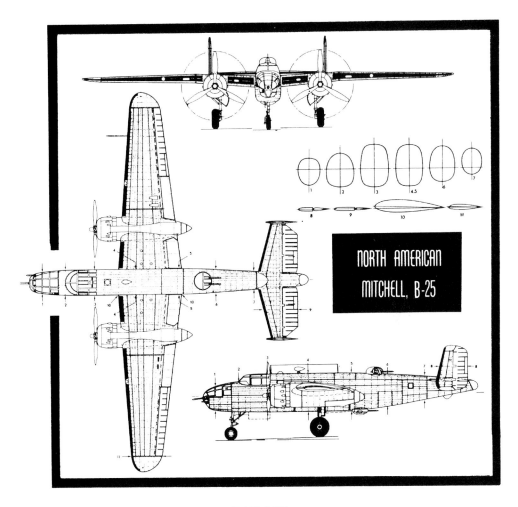

B-25B DATA

Number Built: 120 (one crashed before delivery)
AAF Serial Numbers: 40-2229-40-2242
                       40-2244-40-2348

Span: 67'7"
Wing Area: 610 sq. ft.
Length: 52'11"
Height: 15'9"
Max. Speed: 300 mph @ 15,000'
Normal Bomb Load: 2,400 lbs.
Normal Range: 2,000 miles

Crew: 5
Empty Weight: 20,000 lbs.
Gross Weight: 26,208 lbs. (28,460 max. gross)
Power Plant: 2-1,700 hp 14 cylinder
                 Wright cyclone R-2600-9 engines
                 1,350 hp @ 13,000'

And then the question finally arose: Why? What was the purpose of the B-25C? How would it be employed? What targets would we be expected to hit with minimum altitude strafing and bombing tactics?

The answer: Just about anything that was Japanese, on land and water—grounded aircraft, close air-ground support, convoy interdiction and shipping. Targets we were mostly missing from 10,000 feet. Targets the heavy bombers up at 20,000 feet didn't have even a chance to hit.

Pretty reasonable so far.

But the target list expanded. "Shipping" not only included barges, intercoastal shipping and merchant vessels but also the man-o'-war—especially the destroyers and cruisers that were running supplies and troops to the north coast of New Guinea.

The interest increased but the original enthusiasm evaporated. Strafing and bombing ground targets and intercoastal shipping was doable, but a man-o'-war? Their fully equipped decks of light and heavy guns, their pom-poms, their six inchers would blow us out of the sky. Strafe that? Pull up, clear the mast, slap a bomb into the side and hope to get away?

Morale was slipping badly.

But the determination of General Kenney and Pappy Gunn to put their new weapon to real use overrode the continuing recalcitrance of the pilots who would do the "putting."

Fourteen hundred miles south of our base camp was Eagle Farms at Brisbane, home of this imaginative Pappy Gunn whose crew of mechanics continued creating these radical, scrappy, lethal, low altitude attack planes able to damage and kill extensively and suppress enemy fire while they were at it.

A distinctively remarkable character, a doer with a brain and a reputation for initiating design improvements on the weaponry we were handed, was Paul I. "Pappy" Gunn, an independent cuss, a pioneer in a land and time of pioneers, a man made for the demands of war in a war seemingly made for him.

Most obvious of his several distinguishing characteristics was his age. In his early-to-mid-forties, Pappy was a granddaddy of the fly-boys, caught up in this new war with these new warriors.

Being the old man wasn't enough. On top of his years he had a high, squeaky Arkansas voice, in constant use, mostly to express his well-defined opinions on every subject that arose.

Although I never knew him to lie, he would stretch a point for effect. His stories glistened with detail, real and imagined. He never shortchanged a story for the want of a few facts. He never let the truth interfere with a good tale. His arguments were outlandish but we all learned to be cautious when challenging any of his statements, however wild, because occasionally he produced the proof of his claims.

To prop up his details further, Pappy carried a $1,000 bill in his pants pocket and flipped it out to cover any challenge to his facts. "Put your money where

TEIKOKU KAIJI KYOKAI

The Imperial Japanese Marine Corporation

REPRESENTING

THE BRITISH CORPORATION REGISTER OF SHIPPING AND AIRCRAFT

Tama.

November 30th, 1936.

THIS IS TO CERTIFY that I have surveyed,

on behalf of THE BRITISH CORPORATION REGISTER OF SHIPPING AND AIRCRAFT

Glasgow, the **Steel Screw Steamer " TAIYEI MARU " 3221.04 t**

gross of Tokyo, Off. No. 31357,

and that I have transmitted to the Committee of the said Corporation

Report stating that all repairs recommended by me have been completed

my satisfaction, and that I have recommended that she be **continued as**

classed B.S.* & N.S.* with new record of A.S. 11/1936,

being fit to carry dry and perishable cargoes

Using low level tactics, the planes flew so low that one explosion caused a page from an attacked ship's registry ("Taiyei Maru") to get caught in the engine air intake of one of the planes on a strafing mission.

Col. Paul "Pappy" Gunn in his office—at the controls of his B-25.

your mouth is" often ended any disagreements. That $1,000 bill was part of the Pappy persona until one ill-fated flight up from Eagle Farms to Seven-Mile with Ed Larner and the legendary "Black Jack" Walker, an Australian Group Commander heading up the Thirtieth Squadron, RAAF. Pappy was ministering to a case of crotch rot and was airing his pants out the window of his cockpit when the lid opened and the $1,000 pants flew into the Coral Sea, ending up in the belly of a shark, or the fist of a native.

Pappy served in the Navy during World War I and between wars became a Navy pilot, retiring as a chief petty officer in 1937. He stayed in the Philippines as an active aviator. He was on the team that combed the Pacific looking for

Amelia Earhart when she vanished in the summer of 1937. He had been in commercial aviation, working out of Manila as a private pilot, as a test pilot for the DC-3, instructing flying, operating an inter-island air charter service and supervising maintenance for an island airline. Then the Japanese struck Clark Field.

Now at war, the U.S. commandeered his planes, including his prized twin engine Beechcraft. Including Pappy. He became a 40-something draftee, with a U.S. Army Air Corps pilot's rating and a direct commission as an Army Air Corps captain.

His assignment was ferrying medicines, dispatches, freight shipments and key military and political leaders out of Manila to the southern islands. From there they were evacuating to Australia, avoiding Japanese capture.

Pappy had had an apartment in Manila where he had been living with his wife Polly, two sons and two daughters. The swift and disastrous occupation of Manila in January 1942 separated the Gunns—farther from home and family while Pappy was on a flight to Mindanao, the southernmost island. The Japanese stormed into Manila, taking control of its airports, cutting him off.

Five thousand Manila residents were captured and interned for the war's duration in Santo Tomas, a local Dominican university with dormitory facilities. But Polly and their children were placed under house arrest and questioned repeatedly regarding Pappy's whereabouts. To evade their scrutiny, Polly brought the family to Santo Tomas into the security of numbers. Three years of starvation and sickness passed before Polly and the children were freed by First Calvary tanks rolling into the prison camp in February 1945. Military personnel sought out the Gunn family and flew them to Brisbane for a reunion that opened with Polly saying, "Where have you been for the past three years? And you'd better make it good!"

From Mindanao, the last U.S. holdout in those early days of war, Pappy joined the exodus to Australia, bringing with him his Beechcraft and his instinctive mechanical adroitness. Although not a graduate engineer, he was the genius of jerry-rigging. He envisioned practical applications of machinery and equipment well beyond their original purpose. What didn't work, he could fix. What did work, he made better. What came without instructions, he constructed from an inventory of hidden directions in his head.

Pappy had migrated down to Charters Towers, our Group Headquarters where General George Kenney found him, putting him in charge of the engineering department. His next move was south again, down to Eagle Farms at Brisbane to undertake the modification of the Ninetieth Squadron's B-25s under Kenney's watchful eye.

In spite of our reluctance to take on the powerhouses of the Japanese Navy, as the planes rotated, so did the pilots. During November and December one by one we flew our B-25s down to Brisbane, turned them over to Pappy, bummed around Brisbane playing boulevard commando, treated ourselves to the civilized pleasures of a modern Australian city and when the time came, picked up a converted plane to fly back to Charters Towers.

We wound up 1942 reorganized. The immediate threat to Australia was relieved. We began 1943 with a purpose: push the Japanese back to their homeland. Our weapons were better. Our support was better. We were mentally and physically superior. We were adapting to a new kind of war that created its own tactics. For the Japanese at this point, the war "degenerated into a vicious nightmare in which we struggled hopelessly against a rising enemy tide impossible to overcome." So lamented Saburo Sakai, Japanese fighter ace.

Generals Kenney and Whitehead were putting plans into place that began unfolding. All the first B-25s converted to strafers were assigned to our Ninetieth Squadron, at that early point in the war still based at Charters Towers with the Eighth and Thirteenth Squadrons. The Ninetieth was to be the "Guinea Pig" squadron testing out the new converted weapon and heralded low altitude attack tactics.

As of New Year's Day 1943, the newly organized Ninetieth even had a new leader, Major Ed Larner, transferred from the Thirteenth Squadron and made commander of a team of pilots and crews now equipped with 16 dramatically modified battle-ready low flying aircraft.

I had been promoted to captain the previous October and now was made squadron operations officer to this "hell for leather" combat officer. I could trade my silver bars for doubles. But without a PX to supply my rank insignia to wear on my khakis, Larner resorted to fashioning the bars from white adhesive tape, sticking them on my collar. My first set of captain's bars. By mid-summer I would be a major.

As operations officer I attended all the intelligence briefings, and received specific assignments from bomber command for our 16 planes. My office scheduled those planes by number and crew, kept track of the people keeping those planes in the air, checked out the capabilities of the pilots, assigned the missions and followed up on hits and misses, alerted the maintenance and armament people to ready the planes and arm them according to bomber command orders— 1,000- or 500-pound bombs, 400 rounds of ammunition for each gun. Along with intelligence I debriefed the flight crews. We kept the records on each man, oversaw the medical department so the right pills were in the right places.

Running a squadron of 16 planes is an exacting administrative job. If some of the duties you oversee aren't performed precisely, you get rid of the men who can't produce results and replace them with men who can. These were Larner's and my responsibilities now.

On the back side of my job description was the well-being of my combat crews, the young men far from home, balancing firmness with friendliness. I dressed them down. I backed them up. I kept them in line. I stayed ahead of my men, exposed myself to the greater dangers so they could follow with courage.

My first challenge was none of the above. Gordon was a former Dartmouth football player, a big guy, a good guy. Throughout the winter he had been shuttling our B-25s down to Eagle Farms for conversion. While Pappy was taking out the bomb sights and the lower turret and installing fifty-caliber machine guns in the nose and on the fuselage, Gordon was taking out Sylvia, a beautiful young Indonesian girl in Brisbane. Unfortunately, Sylvia was married to a gun-toting Dutch airline pilot.

On one of my trips down to Brisbane some squadron members alerted me to the problem of a Dutch pilot who was looking for an American officer who was carrying on with his wife. He had vowed to "shoot the son of a bitch."

Here's a job for an operations officer that wasn't covered in the briefings.

I knew who the officer was and I knew when he was scheduled to bring his B-25 down from Charters Towers. So I met him on the airstrip at Eagle Farms. He parked his plane and before he took a step on the tarmac I was in front of him saying "Gordon, there's a Dutch airline captain who has a pistol. He's looking for you and I find out it's quite serious.

"Now we don't want any scandal in our outfit in connection with this. The best, safest thing for you to do is get in that readied plane over there—mine—and take it back to Charters Towers."

Gordon was disappointed. I was interrupting his social life. He offered a list of excuses why he couldn't fly back at that moment.

"Orders, lieutenant. You are going back."

His final plea was "What about my laundry, captain? I've got a laundry ticket here. I have to pick it up." He pulled it from his shirt pocket and waved it in front of me.

I took the chit from his hand to later pick up his clean clothes. Gordon immediately flew my B-25 back to Charters Towers and I brought back his laundry with the next completed B-25.

End of romance.

It was during that period as operations officer that I learned what a personable guy General Kenney was. After the briefings and discussions of squadron assignments, if Kenney were on the base— his actual headquarters were in Brisbane with General MacArthur's—he would come into the meetings, sit down with us and begin talking the night away. He was a pilot with extensive flying time before the Pacific war began. His stories continued well beyond our capacity to pay attention since many of us had been out flying all day. So we would sit in shifts, keeping an audience of three or four guys in attendance while one by one we would slip out for a snooze break and then return. He never missed us or a beat in his tales.

Through all the reorganization and rotation, the concerns about the new battle tactics and the untested expectations of our assigned converted bomber remained.

While the stream of B-25Cs from Eagle Farms at Brisbane proceeded, our new operations home base at Seventeen-Mile was being freshly cut out of the jungle near Durand by engineers, creating a campsite for us and our airplanes. We eventually moved lock, stock and barrel from Australia. That move was our first push north.

Tactic training centered at the entrance to the harbor where the "Moresby Wreck" was the target of choice for our squadron and its converted B-25s. The "Wreck" was a commercial merchant vessel that had been caught in a storm before the war and either by poor navigation or force of weather was left abandoned on a reef. We flew minimum altitude, strafing into it, pulling up to get over the mast and the superstructure of the ship, slapping 100-pound live delayed fuse and practice bombs filled with sand and phosphorous.

I dropped one of those live 100-pounders supposedly fitted with a delayed fuse into the side of the "Wreck." The fuse didn't delay. It went off instantaneously upon impact. WOW! From the jolt I feared that it had done some damage to our plane but all systems were working well—both engines, all gauges "in the green" indicating normal—and I was in full control.

It wasn't until we returned to Seventeen-Mile and landed that we became aware that shrapnel from the bomb had punched holes through the plane, obviously hitting nothing vital.

The crew on board was nonchalant regarding the experience but the crew chief was irate. "What the hell did you do to my airplane, captain?" was his first greeting to me, grumbling that he would be spending too many uncomfortable hours in the revetment patching up all those holes.

I then realized the extent of the damage. Evidently the bomb had penetrated the side of the target ship, exploding below its deck a little earlier than designed, before we were safely away. That ship deck provided our only major protection. As disastrous as the plane looked, the crew had escaped uninjured, thank God. The jeopardy of low level strafing had become a reality.

By early March 1943, the Ninetieth Squadron was fully retrained as highly specialized attack aviators with this exclusive weapon. We were finding satisfaction and gaining confidence in minimum altitude flying. We ran several minor missions against ground targets and night shipping along the south coast of New Britain and the north coast of Papua New Guinea. The strafing was effective; the delayed fuse bombing did quite a job. Our successes continuously proved the power of the refitted B-25. The air battles were becoming increasingly devastating to the enemy.

The main effort the enemy had made during this period was sending a 100-plus plane raid to brighten up one already sunny morning, causing some much needed excitement with very little damage—none to Seventeen-Mile, some to neighboring Seven-Mile and Three-Mile. Our high altitude P-38 Lightnings, the twin-tailed fighters adapted for the South Pacific, had a jamboree.

Top row center and right: E. S. Moser, John Henebry. Bottom row center and right: W. S. Lee, E. T. Dietz in front of "Mary McGuire" (M★M) after repairs to the airplane were completed.

Outside of training and missions, primary attention was given to completion of our new campsite, "Larner's Rock Pile," located on the side of a boulder-laden hill. Every time we drove a tent stake, we hit rock. We had a hell of a time getting positioned.

Interrupting us during that first week of February 1943 came orders intensifying our training for a maximum effort to bring the crew to peak proficiency and all planes in commission. A feeling pervaded that something was going to happen. And it did—the Battle of the Bismarck Sea.

Late in the afternoon of March 2, Larner and I were called to Fifth Bomber Command for a briefing, along with officer representatives of all the A-20, B-25, B-17, B-24 Liberator squadrons and the Australian Beaufighter squadron fighting with us.

An unusual gathering. Never before had all squadrons been represented at a briefing at one time. Quickly, the briefing officer got to the point. From B-17 recon and radio intercepts, Fifth Air Force learned that a newly formed Japanese convoy, launched from Rabaul Harbor under cover of bad weather, was proceeding in a westerly direction down the north coast of New Britain. An estimated 22 ships—seven merchant ships, six destroyers and two cruisers joined en route by seven additional merchant vessels—were proceeding on a 400-mile voyage toward either Lae or Salamaua (tucked in the Huon Gulf), to resupply and strengthen the beleaguered Japanese troops with an additional 7,000 soldiers and supplies. Their exact destination would not be determined until later that night, perhaps not even until the following morning.

In the meantime, we assumed one of these two coastal towns to be their goal. Sure enough, the next morning, March 3rd, we received word that the convoy, covered by land-based air protection, had turned south out of the Bismarck Sea after passing Cape Gloucester and was heading for the Vitiaz Straits.

This was a full force operation. The briefing instructions had all units, everything the Fifth Air Force, including its P-38 fighter cover, and the RAAF could get airborne, rendezvous over Cape Ward Hunt, proceed north and intercept the convoy as it came through the strait between New Britain and New Guinea. As programmed, 12 strafing B-25Cs of the Ninetieth were flying for the first time as low level bombers below and behind the medium altitude B-25s and the high level B-17s and B-24s.

Some 45 minutes after the Cape Ward Hunt rendezvous, we saw the first action. At high altitude the P-38s were defending us against Japanese fighters. So effective were they through this and the following day of combat that not once during the three missions against this moving target were we attacked by Japanese fighters from above.

The P-38s at last had wrested control of the air away from the Japanese, even the air over their own airstrips. We were exhausting this once invincible air power—their supplies and equipment, their first line of pilots. We now dominated the skies.

Minutes after witnessing the fighter action, we saw the convoy. Unfortunately for the Japanese, it materialized distinctly, the weather being clear and our visibility unlimited—a CAVU day.

What a picture! A convoy of light cruisers, destroyers, freighters, troop transports and merchant vessels was indeed heading for Lae.

The crews in our squadron were apprehensive about the impending confrontation. Here for the first time we were sighting the real thing—an enemy man-o'-war protecting ships carrying troop reinforcements, key personnel and vital fuel, food and other supplies to New Guinea. Here for the first time we were seriously about to employ a radical tactic with a newly converted weapon—tactics and weapons that had never been combined before. Anxious and apprehensive were we.

Larner and his "Spook II" led our formation of 12 converted B-25s now flying at about 2,000 feet. I was flying wing position along side him. He started his descent several miles from the convoy. We had followed him down to the surface when he broke radio silence and announced on our squadron frequency, "I'm making a run on that lead cruiser. You guys pick out your own targets." And he made a slight left turn into the gunfire from the convoy.

About a mile from his target, approaching it broadside, he opened up his machine gun fire. Then, to our amazement, the guns on the ships stopped firing back at him. A B-25's barrage of fifty-caliber gunfire certainly will send the

Major Ed Larner in his B-25 *"Spook II"*

enemy scurrying. When you get those guns on their decks quickly, overwhelming their defenses there, you catch them exposed waist high. They duck and you can kill, injure or confuse whoever is manning those threatening guns. Survivors may return to their positions in time to reload for another crack at you but for the brief moment after your opening fire their guns are still. That moment allows you to come in for the kill with your bombs.

Larner kept strafing in close and as he pulled up to clear the masts, he slapped his 500-pounders into the ship. At least one, maybe two or three of his bombs smashed into the side.

Japanese destroyer under attack, Bismarck Sea

As he climbed away on the other side of the ship the four- to five-second delayed fuse bombs caused a gigantic explosion that engulfed the cruiser. It rolled afloat while fire and smoke poured out. Later it sank.

This sight, in this instant, of this courageous leader in action set a tremendous example for all to see. Our first successful hit from minimum altitude was confirmation that General Kenney's, and before him, Brigadier General Billy Mitchell's, controversial theory of "attack aviation" against enemy shipping was sound.

Some 20 years before this day the legendary independent air power advocate,

Brigadier General Billy Mitchell, spoke often and loudly and dissentingly about the inability of sea-bound surface vessels to survive hostile air attacks, that enemy ships traveling within range of land-based aircraft would be doomed. The warplane could be the new dimension of warfare. And here was Larner's North American Aviation B-25—the Mitchell bomber—playing a prominent role in realizing the controversial prophecy.

Larner's run had instilled in his initially skeptical squadron pilots, and I was included among the doubtful, an immediate confidence in this new tactic. "What the hell," we thought, "if he can do that, so can we." Thus sustained, we each picked a ship and went after it. I made three low level runs, attacking a damaged destroyer and two transports.

We ran two bombing missions against that convoy on March 3rd and one more on March 4th to finish off anything that was left.

The entire convoy was sunk by the time we had finished. Flotsam off the ships stretched for three miles. Nothing got ashore. No one survived our guns. Land-based medium-altitude and our low-altitude B-25s, Beaufighters, B-17s and A-20s had done the devastating job. Larner's maiden attack had proved the potency of low flying B-25s and established them as a deadly threat to any enemy shipping within our range. No Japanese troops, equipment or supplies reached their destination on the day that marked the beginning of the end of the war. The battle ended Japanese attempts to use convoys to support their troops and it ended Japanese control of the Vitiaz Straits, a path our ships needed in our move to the Philippines.

Sinking an entire seagoing convoy of merchant and war ships and downing some 60 of their fighter planes using only land-based aircraft was a military milestone. The victory in the Bismarck Sea was the first defeat of such a large naval force achieved without the use of Navy surface vessels. Because the targets included military vessels and transports, the victory denied the Japanese control over New Guinea, stifling the continuation of the original offensive to isolate or invade Australia. Abandonment was their only available alternative.

For us it was the beginning of a highly successful phase of the Southwest Pacific war. We carried into subsequent battles that vision of our great aerial victory over an enemy convoy caught without adequate defenses against a storm of B-25s unexpectedly blasting, bombing and sinking their ships. We had proven a tactic designed for the distant isolated targets of the Pacific. Thereafter we believed in low level attack and stuck to those tactics, accomplishing our missions skillfully.

That our total victory was a major turning point in the war was acknowledged as such by MacArthur and other world military leaders.

The enemy's failure to reach Lae was also symbolic. The Japanese were over-extended. Military elements in the homeland were in control of the government and had over-committed the country in the face of the sleeping giant's arousal.

Seventeen-Mile Airstrip, March 1943. Ninetieth Squadron of the Third Attack Group crews who participated in Bismarck Sea first strike, the morning of March 3, 1943, another strike that same evening and a third strike the morning of March 4. Maj. Ed Larner (center, with cap, standing), the Squadron Commanding Officer, Capt. John Henebry (on Larner's right), the Squadron Operations Officer. First Lt. Bob Chatt (on Larner's left), with Chatt's B-25 "Chatter Box" in the background.

Later intelligence pointed to a growing desire at this time to dig in and attempt negotiations toward a peace settlement.

Word of the success of our contrived war machine reached Wright Field. Swiftly, engineers at North American Aviation, the designer and manufacturer of the B-25, brought their slide rules and rolls of drawings to Eagle Farms to inspect this home-made conversion of their masterpiece aircraft. The thought of local boys tinkering with their tightly engineered bomber was unthinkable. Preposterous.

Pappy gathered them around, explaining the conversion he had been masterminding over the past six months.

Then he put them in "Margaret" and flew them around the Coral Sea reminding them of the definitive victory the B-25 brought to the Bismarck Sea. They flew the planes low; they fired the guns; they were impressed. Without question our B-25s were proving their worth in the belligerent Pacific skies. Low. On top of the action.

"But," they mused, "this airplane is dangerous. With all the guns and ammunition in the nose, you have too much weight forward, too far ahead of the designated center of gravity. Where's your center of gravity?"

"Center of gravity?" Pappy answered. "Hell, we took that out to lighten the ship and sent it back to Air Corps Supply."

The Battle of the Bismarck Sea did more than sink a lot of Japanese ships. It woke up a lot of people in the Pentagon and the White House to the real war going on the Southwest Pacific area. It became obvious what wonders Lieutenant General George Kenney and his Far East Air Force were accomplishing with restricted personnel and equipment.

While the Allied Navy should be complimented for the pounding it had been handing out, the war in the Pacific had become more than a Navy war. After the Bismarck Sea scrap, more equipment, air crews, ground forces and engineers, capable of building more air bases, became available.

After the Bismarck Sea, enough planes arrived to bring us up to strength. We had been down to 12 of an authorized 16 B-25s. Soon all four of our squadrons each had 16, converted into attack aircraft and ready for combat—against enemy airdromes, interdicting enemy supply lines, providing close air support of Army and Marine ground forces and amphibian landings. Even the original, leftover, worn-out A-20s of the Eighty-Ninth Squadron were replaced with B-25s. We were up to strength by August 17, 1943, when we led our attack on a new, fresh Japanese air armada, to wipe it out at Wewak.

Nineteen forty-three, it was a very good year. I flew in every big strike the Third made. By year end we had secured Australia, leapfrogged over New Britain and Papua New Guinea and were moving over Dutch New Guinea, chasing the Japanese back to the Philippines.

By the end of 1943 the Mitchell bomber had played out its part. Attack aviation had made history. By the end of 1943 new aircraft was replacing the workhorse of the Southwest Pacific as designers created lighter, speedier aircraft, capable of delivering bombs and bullets on a waning enemy.

But Pappy worked on, and then returned home to the Philippines after the war ended. He eventually died there. Putting him in his final resting place was as complicated a scenario as was his life.

His wife Polly's permanent residence was now Pensacola, Florida. She and their family wanted to bring his corpse there for burial. One night Doc Gilmore's Santa Monica phone rang. On the other end was the commanding officer of Travis Air Force Base 80 miles north of San Francisco. "We've got a body up here with your name on it." The Gunn boys had conned someone in Manila to put it aboard a Military Air Transport plane and ship it to San Francisco in care of Dr. John Gilmore, now a reserve Air Force colonel. Pappy, at the time of his death, had no military status. He was long out of the service and had settled again in the Philippines as a civilian, ultimately becoming vice president of Philippine Airlines. In true Pappy Gunn style, the body was traveling unauthorized, incognito, without orders, contrary to all regulations in an unmarked shipping case.

Doc's response was to suggest that the officer forward the shipment on down to Florida where burial plans were supposed to be in the making.

"No," the officer replied, "this body doesn't move without you."

After a couple of days of futile long-distance arguing Doc contacted me, by that time a reserve brigadier general back in the Midwest. I in turn arranged for a twin-engine airplane to be sent from a reserve unit in Oklahoma City to pick up the body at Travis. Doc met me and the Oklahoma City plane there, arriving about midnight. Out of spite, he called the commanding general at that hour asking, "Where are my orders to take this body to Pensacola?"

His response was, "There aren't any orders. You're on your own . . ."

So we loaded the body aboard the reserve plane taking it back to Oklahoma City, changed airplanes there and proceeded to Pensacola. The only food we had was a boxed lunch prepared for us in Oklahoma City.

Once in Pensacola we ran into the complications of burial. Polly was a staunch Catholic insisting on a Catholic burial. Pappy was a Mason. Arranging a dispensation ate up time. But finally what resulted was Pappy Gunn's burial as a retired Air Force officer in a Naval burial plot in a Catholic cemetery with an Air Force gun salute. My fear was that the holy water would sizzle when the Catholic chaplain sprinkled it over the casket.

But as Doc eulogized: "This was the way Pappy lived all his life—as the Master of Confusion."

Col. Paul "Pappy" Gunn

8

Jungle Living

NINETEEN FORTY-THREE had opened rather quietly. The Japanese were not very active the winter of '42–43 and consequently, our responses were minimal. Two, three, then four weeks passed without a target assignment coming down to us. What the hell was going on, we wondered, unused to silent skies. We would fantasize that the Japanese had gone home until the occasional Japanese recon plane, "Bed Check Charlie," flew over to spy on our activities. Then we knew the war was still on.

Winston Churchill, Franklin Delano Roosevelt and Australian Prime Minister John Curtin were arguing about who should be fighting where. A primary concern in our niche in the world was the three divisions of Australian troops assigned in North Africa. Curtin wanted them pulled back home. He wanted his own men defending their very vulnerable country. The memory of the Allied sacrifice of the Philippines loomed large and he intended that Australians join the U.S. and Dutch troops as Australia's primary defenders.

By September 1942 we had started to see the results of the Army Corps of Engineers' efforts at airstrip construction to house the Third's increasing numbers of bombers and eventually P-38s. Through the fall, without facilities on New Guinea, we had been shuttling the three and a half hour flight between Charters Towers in Australia and Port Moresby on the southern coast of New Guinea to launch air strikes against Wirope on the Kokoda Trail, the north coast of New Guinea and all of New Britain.

Finally Port Moresby's Eleven-Mile and then Seventeen-Mile, our eventual home, materialized allowing two more of our three squadrons remaining at Charters Towers to follow the Eighty-Ninth which had been based in New Guinea since August 1942. The Eighth remained as maintenance backup while it continued waiting for planes. Eventually even that squadron was reunited with a complete Third Attack Group in Papua New Guinea.

We would now be staging in unison through Seventeen-Mile at Durand with 5,000 feet of runway, 17 miles northwest of Port Moresby. This new field was an improvement over the original Port Moresby strip—Seven-Mile at Jackson—crowded with a growing inventory of American personnel and equipment.

We were getting up to strength in our converted B-25 strafers and establishing our camps nearby. We continued training in recon and low level strafing and bombing on the empty and abandoned "Moresby Wreck" in the bay.

The move to Seventeen-Mile as an operating base brought classic problems of frontier expansion—the raw primitive jungle imposed intolerable living conditions upon us. We had the down time to appreciate our sorry lot. This was a wild land, not designed for civilized man, home to spiders, scorpions, centipedes, lizards, snakes and, to balance their horror, beautiful jungle birds.

First Operations Center for the Ninetieth Squadron at Seventeen-Mile Airstrip

Contending with crocodiles became an occupation. The engineers had cut off a bend in the river outside Port Moresby to create land for the airfield. The cut left behind a big pond about 50 feet wide and a mile long. A permanent home to crocks who had been used to going with the flow of the river. Those massive animals who are able to run as fast as a horse would invade our camps at night, mad and hungry. Shooting crocodiles became sport.

In order to disperse our planes and ourselves into the thicket to protect them and us from possible enemy air attack, the Army engineers constructed airplane parking revetments—hard stands—in the brush, remote from the runway. To reach them, of course, we needed taxiways to each assigned airplane parking space.

In contrast to the runway at Seven-Mile, straight, leveled and sealed with a combination of pierced steel plank and black top, these taxiways looped around through the jungle to the individual revetments. They were gravel. They were unsealed. And the air was filled with thick red dust stirred up by a moving plane's propellers. with a heavy bomb load on, a plane at takeoff would cause an upheaval that obliterated the view.

The frequent rains of New Guinea's south coast often relieved the problem, dampening down the dust, and we always welcomed them. The rains flowed off the main runway, the taxiways and the revetments, all properly constructed to

Sgt. Miller, a crew chief with the Ninetieth Squadron, at Seventeen-Mile Airstrip early living quarters

prevent standing water. However, that water flowed into the land adjacent to the revetments where we had pitched our tents, claiming that land as our living space.

High temperatures and standing water equal fungi and mosquitos. We had it all. The mosquito population at Seventeen-Mile surpassed any bug population I ever lived with through all my ensuing years in the Pacific theater. The annoyance of the buzzing and biting of the anopheles mosquito was minor, of course, to the threat of malaria and dengue fever this insect presented. To this day malaria remains a serious, life threatening disease and dengue—red bone fever with its aching bones—remains without a vaccine and without a cure.

The mosquitos were everywhere except in the direct tropical sun and in our cockpits. Mosquitos stuck with the protective jungle shade. The cleanliness, the lack of residue and absence of water inside our bombers made that area also less attractive to mosquitos than our swampland living quarters.

For immediate relief then we stood in the sun. Our ultimate relief was to escape into the skies. The air washed away any bug hangers-on. Free and clean, it was truly a deliverance to fly. Our major consolation was that we weren't fighting through the mud as were the ground-pounders currently in combat at bloody Buna, across the Owen Stanley Range, who were dealing with the rain, the heat, the mosquitos and water snakes in combination with a ferocious enemy battling inch by inch for a northern coast stronghold.

In good times our laundry would be done by native kids until the Australia-New Guinea Administrative Unit, the ANGAUs, hauled them off to perform more legitimate chores for the Allies. Then we were on our own, constructing wash tanks from halved 55-gallon drums hoisted over fires, using long poles to stir our clothes clean.

We slept on the infamous army cots in eight-man squad tents, generally in a few inches of stagnant water. The bedtime ritual was a project. After tucking in mosquito netting all around the cot, the next step, armed with a flashlight and spray can of insecticide, was to dispatch the few stalwart mosquitos whose fate placed them within the arranged netting.

One of the more practical inventions of World War II was the air mattress. Not too different from the variety now offered as guest beds for unexpected company, our jungle variety was also self-inflatable, but with greater exertion demanded on our part. The narrow mattress, designed to fit on top of the narrow cot, came equipped with a casing. To inflate the mattress, you captured air in the case and squeezed it into the mattress through a one-way valve. Six, seven, eight times around and the mattress was full.

The singular benefit of the air mattress to us—probably more important than its obvious comfort factor—was that now we could tuck the mosquito netting between it and the cot canvas, making our primary defense against mosquitos more secure.

The only airman who didn't relish the introduction of the air mattress was David

Capt. John "Robbie" Robinson getting his laundry done at Seventeen-Mile Airstrip

McComber, one of our crewmen, a brilliant but rather disjointed navigator and later a professor at Bowdoin College, who chose simply to wrap his body in his mosquito netting rather than perform the nightly draping and tucking rituals.

The nights we were forced to spend in the trenches, often in the company of lizards, protecting ourselves from potential bombing raids, made us appreciate the mattresses and netting even more.

Bite preventing mosquito netting, bug sprays, protective clothing—we were always required to wear long trousers and long-sleeved shirts—and medications—quinine, quinine tablets dissolved in sulfuric acid served with orange juice and eventually a new drug, atabrine—somewhat controlled malaria and its 100-plus degree fevers and dysentery. Controlled but not conquered, the diseases remained a problem throughout the war for the New Guinea fighters and for GIs throughout the Pacific Theater.

Our early mess hall

Yet, through three and a half years of constant exposure, I contracted neither malaria nor dengue. The trots, called "the GIs," yes.

If the bugs didn't getcha, the food would. Food poisoning was another major health problem. In our tropical temperatures, without refrigeration (as we were in the initial periods of our New Guinea encampments), food spoiled at fast-forward speed.

Refrigeration finally came on the rear end of a truck. In true frontier style, mechanics had designed a storage unit to fit on a truck bed and deposited it with an accompanying energy unit near the mess.

The coolers put us in the gourmet food business. Where even canned meat had a short life in our original time at Seventeen–Mile, we now were seeing fresh cuts. With buddies who had buddies and with one deal hinging on another, line chiefs and mess sergeants doing for each other, stretching back into the caches of Australia, we were seeing some respectable refrigerated food in our tented mess hall.

Sitting around our revetment at Seventeen-Mile in the shade of our B-25 wing, we toasted the resourcefulness of our crew chief, Tech Sergeant Al Deemie.

It was he who kept our plane in shape ready to go, always on the ready. Deemie was regular Army before there was a World War II. He was good Midwestern stock, raised during the Depression near Peoria, Illinois. He had more angles than a maze.

We toasted him with Foster beer, available through his wile. This classic Australian beer was bottled in hefty half-gallon bottles. We never questioned how, but during our shuttles back and forth to Charters Towers, Deemie always managed to bring aboard a few bottles on the return trip to the island. At Seventeen-Mile we never could chill it to stateside standards but the beer was a welcome treat at any temperature.

Canned hams, candy and cookies also appeared, the result of Deemie's operations. He was one of the best.

There were other ways to acquire basic foods. Pappy Gunn, who had no respect for military regulations and had an uncanny ability to see needs and fill them, needed a cup of coffee. The whole of Charters Towers seemed to have run out of the bean. Pappy heard that the quartermaster was stashing away a supply and Pappy went after it. The quartermaster insisted he had none. Pappy pulled out his .45 and walked away with his supply.

Because of the rough and rugged discomforts of our primitive equatorial life, our great escape was to load up the combat crew, the ground maintenance crew and the mechanics assigned to our plane and fly the 600 miles south over the Coral Sea to our base at Charters Towers.

What we relished as civilization there was nothing but the outgrowth of an abandoned gold mining town from a century previous, sitting on the rim of a semi-arid wilderness. Wartime austerity had struck hard and creature comforts were minimal. We lived in tents at Charters Towers too but the weather, much like Tucson's, the physical environment and the food were better than in the tropics of New Guinea.

And here, safely in Australia, the Japanese were not a mere 30 miles away, hovering beyond the Kokoda Pass.

We often ran into bad flying weather when shuttling down to Charters Towers. An alternate airstrip available to us when it was better to be on the ground was a sleek 5,000-foot black-top runway at the little tropical seaside town of Cairns on the Queensland coast about 250 miles north of Charters Towers, a town that served as the hub of a sugar plantation system.

On one such flight south in December 1942, as we approached the Queensland coast, the weather turned sticky. It was late in the afternoon and because we were flying without any navigational aids such as radio communications, homing beacons or lights, I put into Cairns, the closest alternate available.

We landed and reported in to our squadron headquarters by land lines. The timing was wise. This active weather front was not clearing. We were to be stuck in Cairns for two days and three nights.

This was a hiatus in which we could forget war. We found a small but clean hotel, yet comfortable. The weather would have been intolerable to an ordinary visitor to Cairns, but to us it was a gift from heaven.

Sleep and blackjack filled those days and nights. Between rain showers, Lieutenant Pop Hicks and I walked around this beautiful little town sandwiched between sugar cane and the sea. It was a calming period, totally lacking in the intensity of the months of air combat we had survived.

During one of our foot excursions onto the streets of Cairns, we came upon a warehouse and struck up a conversation with a gentleman who was its manager, Mr. Borland.

These Australians in Cairns, like Australians we had met elsewhere, were very friendly. At this time and in this place they were especially hospitable because only a few months before, during the four-day battle of the Coral Sea in May, the fear of Japanese invasion had become particularly real. A joint force of American Navy and Australian warships intercepted an enemy fleet and halted its advance on Port Moresby as a stepping stone to Australia. The battle had ended and the focus shifted as I was aboard ship coming into this theater. Darwin, at the northern edge of Australia, had suffered a bombing the year before. Earlier, midget subs had raided Sydney and Newcastle on the southeastern shore. Australians had become acutely appreciative of all "Yanks" being there now to help keep the enemy at a more comfortable distance.

Hicks, by nature also a very friendly person, now in a very friendly land, commented enthusiastically about the beauty of the town and complimented the gentleman on the hospitality of its people. As if to prove us right, he hosted us at a tasteful, if simple, lunch at a small nearby restaurant.

Naturally, during the lunch conversation the subject of wartime shortages came up, specifically the inadequacies in the supply of that necessity of life: whiskey. Mr. Borland agreed that yes, there were many problems confronting the population, but reiterated that living conditions would be considerably more uncomfortable if the "Yanks" had not come along to help out in the country's defense. How grateful his townspeople were for the Yanks.

He confided in us that a seacoast port town, even this one with its recent scare of Japanese invasion, was luckier than most other Australian locales, especially the Outback and inland towns like our Charters Towers.

We expanded on our complaint that at our home base everything was scarce, even food, but most noticeable was the lack of beer and whiskey.

Mr. Borland made no comment regarding our deprivations but felt that if we could come by his office the next morning he might see what he could do to ease our critical shortages. We assured our new, sympathetic best friend that we would be by to see him. We kept our promise.

What a morning. Unbelievable! Mr. Borland had mysteriously located a shipment of Scotch whiskey that had been stored in his warehouse and magically convinced its owner that he should sell us a portion of it.

He apologized that as much as he wanted to, he couldn't give it to us, that he would have to charge us a wholesale "bulk" price.

We agreed, buying was fine by us, thinking we were negotiating for a bottle or two. He said the "bulk" was five imperial gallons in an all-wooden keg with a wooden spigot— 25 fifths for, as I remember, 60 or 70 Australian pounds.

We rushed back to our hotel, confiscated the blackjack ante and emptied our pockets to raise the money. We borrowed a Jeep and drove back to the warehouse in record time, picked up the keg and delivered it to the airstrip where we sequestered it in our plane, secured it with our own crew members as guards, judged the weather flyable, filed a flight clearance and departed for Charters Towers. By morning takeoff the weather was miraculously no longer an issue. It was remarkably clear.

Hicks and I were proud of this deal. It had out-Deemied Al Deemie. We were heroes to our squadron.

Back at Charters Towers, Captain Don McNutt assumed the position of bar keeper. Our "Officers Club" was a tent with a canvas canopy out front. The "bar" was created from two empty upright steel 55-gallon gasoline drums with a wood plank stretched between. McNutt rigged up a display table behind the "bar" where he enthroned the keg of scotch with the wood spigot positioned for action.

Left to right: Rowland, Norton, Randerson, and Don McNutt

76

From this pinnacle he rationed the precious contents with the authority and aplomb of an officiating cardinal. He was miserly and just. The contents lasted several days.

Captain Scott Dennison, our Thirteenth Squadron adjutant, had a friend, Captain John Gilmore, then the newly arrived flight surgeon of the neighboring squadron and known to have a taste for scotch. As soon as the keg was tapped, Scott departed quietly in a Jeep and returned shortly with Doc Gilmore in tow.

And thus we, Doc Gilmore and I, through the war and to this day, toast Mr. Borland and the long lasting friendship his generosity produced. I quote "Black Jack" Walker, "There's only one decent thing that happens during a war: you make some very fine friends."

9

A Moonlit Miss

THE moon was full May 15, 1943.

A radio intercept informed First Air Task Force operations that a Japanese submarine would be surfacing in the Lae Harbor at dark. First Air wanted it sunk.

First Air, the advanced echelon of the Fifth Air Force, Brigadier General Freddy Smith commanding, had just set up shop after Allied ground forces had secured Dobodura, down 175 miles of New Guinea's north coast from Lae. Our Ninetieth Squadron/ Third Attack Group was still based at Seventeen-Mile near Port Moresby, on the southern side of New Guinea, a mountain range away.

We received a call to send five B-25s over to Dobodura that afternoon, to prepare for a special mission against the submarine that night. Major Ed Larner, Ninetieth Squadron commander, assigned the lead to me as the squadron's operations officer.

I took four of our best pilots including Captains Chuck Howe, one of the coolest cookies in the air, and red-headed Don MacLellan, one of the best combat pilots the war ever produced. They had impressive combat records and were excellent formation fliers. They could tuck their wings close in directly behind me and stay with me through the fight.

Our five B-25s took off late that afternoon, flew the 35 minute flight over the Owen Stanley Range and landed at one of Dobodura's two new airstrips. Major Francis Gideon, a flying school classmate of mine assigned to operations at the First Air Task Force, met us at the airfield.

We reviewed the obvious goal of the assignment. It was up to us to figure out how to make it happen.

The town of Lae is an easy navigational mark. It sits in a corner of the Huon Gulf where the coastline angles due east. We also had the wide Markham River flowing southeast down from the Highlands, emptying into the Gulf.

From top left clockwise: Don MacLellan, Bridges, Hornburger, and Lott

Other prime landmarks were mountain ranges to the north, southwest and east. Historically, Lae was significant to airmen because it had been the last known takeoff for Amelia Earhart on her fatal attempted around-the-world flight less than a decade before.

Our most precise landmark was the "Lae Wreck," the prow of a sunken freighter sticking straight up out of the harbor water at the end of the Lae runway.

At this stage of the war Lae, with its airstrip and harbor, was one of three major Japanese bases still supplying a desperately savage fight to hold control of New Guinea conquests. Our outfit, and others, had been running air strikes against it for more than a year.

We decided upon a night strike. To guarantee the surprise factor, we couldn't be near Lae in daylight. If our targeted submarine had a mere hint that our planes were in the area, it could crash dive and surely would be under water by the time we arrived.

This mission needed to be a night mission. The sub would be surfaced then and we probably wouldn't run into fighter aircraft opposition after dark since the Japanese pilots weren't very adept at night fighting. I knew of no fighter interceptions after dark in the several months I had been based on New Guinea.

And too, their fighter aircraft population was fairly well diminished from the extensive daylight raids the heavy bombers and our B-25s had been running. We had been hitting them hard for a couple of months, trying to clear enemy planes out of the territory.

So the challenge was flying in close and making a run on the sub without being detected. We really wanted the valuable surprise factor.

The full moon at our backs could make us very visible. So an approach from the east was out. We also didn't want to fly over Salamaua or Wau, south of Lae, where Japanese ground forces were abundant and effective. Approaching from the west with the dark mountain at our backs would minimize our visibility.

Flying out of Dobodura then, we headed northwest, skirting the coastline. The night was clear. Visibility was excellent. A few miles past Cape Ward Hunt we descended to under 100 feet above the water and proceeded northwesterly up the coast, working a little farther out to sea as we approached Salamaua on a thin peninsula of land extending some two miles into the Huon Gulf. By reading the mountains to the west, we were aware of Salamaua's proximity.

We were 25 miles south of our objective, just past the treacherous peninsula, when we lowered to under 50 feet and turned west to make a landfall between Salamaua and the mouth of the Markham River, turning north to hit the river dead straight ahead.

At the mouth of the Markham River, turning to the right toward the harbor—there she was. Two miles ahead, surfaced, not more than 200 yards offshore, nose toward Lae, providing us the ideal full broadside run.

A cinematographer could not have created a more effective scene. Five B-25s flying straight and quiet along the coastline toward a surfaced Japanese submarine, silhouetted against a rising full moon.

The waters were alive with activity. Workers unloading the submarine. Small boats plying between the sub and the shore.

A mile from our target I started lobbing fifty-caliber fire onto the sub. The shore batteries started firing at us at the same time. Bomb bay door open, I continued strafing the conning tower and the scurrying boats nearby. All five planes in unison strafed and prepared to drop bombs.

I dropped all four of my 500-pound bombs to lay a string across the sub, pulled up to clear the mast and got back down on the deck.

And then I was hit. A tremendous thump. But the plane was running good. No problem with control. Perhaps whatever had hit us didn't do extensive damage. Whatever had connected created too big a thump to be a hit from the offshore batteries. We figured one of our own 500-pounders had skipped over the sub and tried to fly formation with us until its four- to five-second delayed fuse ignited. The blast of a 500-pound bomb in midair has impact for quite a distance.

Bombs unloaded on a significant target, damaged from unknown fire but flying well, I turned with the others to climb out over the Owen Stanley Range directly to our Seventeen-Mile home base. The flight was somber; we had lost one airman, Sergeant Hume, a gunner for one of my wingmen, shot and killed by the shore batteries.

For what? Had we sunk the sub? We were confident that we had and went to bed thinking so. But the coast watchers couldn't confirm the sinking and later reports had it limping out of the harbor after an aborted harbor stop, considerably damaged by our 10,000 pounds of bombs.

Wewak

THE war progressed to a second summer. The Japanese military had not been able to accomplish either facet of its war plan. The cursed white man's presence was growing. Trade routes to the homeland were everywhere in jeopardy. The entire Pacific adventure was turning against these ill-fated warriors.

Since their total turn back defeat in the Coral Sea in the spring of 1942 preventing their establishing a stronghold on New Guinea's underbelly, they had absorbed continual and serious setbacks. The 100-ship Japanese fleet suffered a debilitating defeat at the hands of the Navy at Midway Island in June. Allies recaptured Guadalcanal and secured Milne Bay. The U.S. reinforced Port Moresby while tough, heroic Australian land forces halted the insane effort to reach that strategic city overland via the Kokoda mountain trail. Vicious ground fighting over Buna was ending in Allied success. Then finally, the ignominy of the Bismarck Sea battle. Lost battle layered upon lost battle.

The Allies were threatening Salamaua, Lae, Finschhafen, the entire north coast of Papua New Guinea, Cape Gloucester, the Admiralty Islands. Finally in sight was New Britain with the focus on Rabaul.

By August 1943, the Japanese were determined to hold what remained. To do so, they had to concentrate their widespread army and naval forces to oppose MacArthur's powerful, determined northwestward push toward the Philippines.

We on the line didn't know it at the time but headquarters had been reading Japanese mail. Code-breaking intelligence experts were able to warn General George Kenney and his Fifth Air Force of detected enemy plans to strengthen air power on the coast of New Guinea.

A look at a map told Kenney that, to be effective, the Japanese needed their air bases as close as Wewak on a stretch of land in the shadows of the Alexander Range on the north Papuan coast. This wild mountain country protected the flat coastal areas to its north. Like Rabaul on the northeast tip of New Britain,

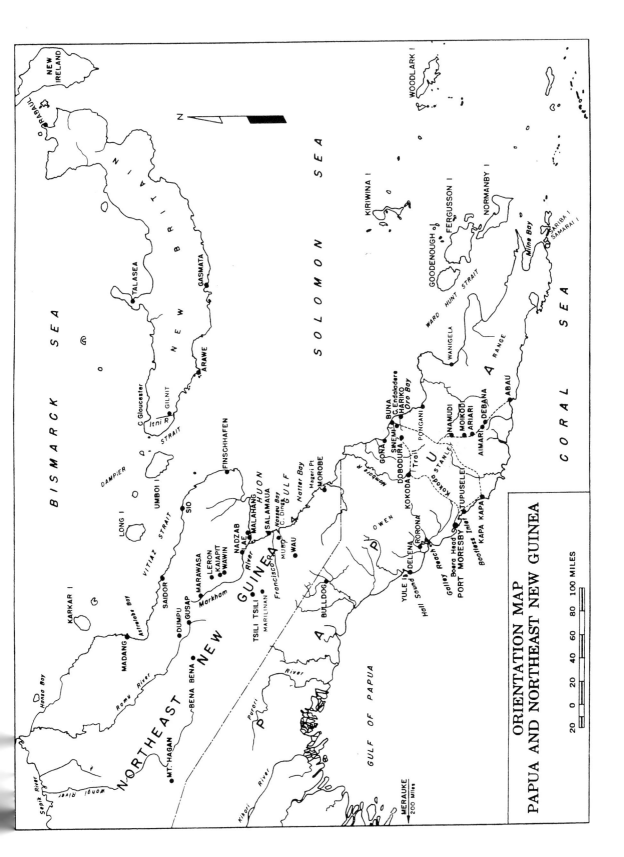

ORIENTATION MAP
PAPUA AND NORTHEAST NEW GUINEA

Wewak would be a strategic airfield complex and staging base for Japanese air power brought in to support the 100,000-strong ground forces trying to stave off burgeoning American and Australian advances in New Guinea. At Wewak, four dusty airstrips gave them facilities to launch light and heavy bombers and fighter craft.

Wewak was 500 miles northwest of our newly established Third Attack Group base at Dobodura, well beyond the range of what had now become Kenney's favorite weapon—our low level strafing B-25.

The distance was a major problem, solved by "Uncle" George's fertile mind and his determination to put the B-25 to its ultimate use.

As delivered from the U.S., the factory model B-25 had a powered machine gun turret in the lower rear fuselage. We removed it in the field as unnecessary protection for minimum altitude tactics since we were flying so low no fighter could attack from underneath. Instead we had the fifty-calibers in the nose. Kenney now envisioned a 300-gallon gasoline tank in the space where the lower gun turret had been. The length of our missions was solely dependant upon the range of our aircraft, its primary factor being available fuel. Gasoline on board gave us more time in the air, more distance.

That concept was only the beginning of the solution. Where in the world, and especially the South Pacific, could we accumulate enough tanks to install in the 84 B-25s scheduled to hit Wewak?

Kenney's plan of course was, "We'll make them in Australia." Didn't he have Pappy Gunn, his gadgeteering wonder worker who could produce upon demand with limited resources?

Could they be self-sealing and leak-proof? Full or empty, would they be safe to have aboard the B-25s?

"No," Kenney admitted. "But we can slip them into the lower fuselage and burn off that added fuel during the unhampered first two hours of flight. Then, we'll drop the tanks on the way to the target before we are in combat and eliminate the fire hazard from enemy fire or crash landings."

This plan sprouted from the same Massachusetts Institute of Technology–trained mind that had delivered trucks to the Buna campaign in 1942. When the ground troops fighting that tough battle needed vehicles too cumbersome to fit into a C-47, then our largest transport plane moving materiel over the Owen Stanley Range, Kenney instructed his ground crews to "get the torches, cut them in half, put the pieces into the C-47, fly them over the mountains landing as close as you can to Buna. Then unload the cargo and weld the parts back together again." That's what his men did and it worked. Resourceful imagination.

So down in Townsville and Brisbane Australia, Kenney had Pappy's mechanics fabricate square 300-gallon tanks from locally produced flat rolled steel. They added hooks on top similar to those on the bombs we carried.

Then they cut a square hole in the bottom of each B-25. On either side they

Conditions were substantially improved for the Third Attack Group airmen when they moved to Dobodura

fastened doors, spring loaded with steel springs—the kind I remember from my grandmother's screen door.

As guide rails and to keep the tank from moving in flight, they mounted four angle irons. The corners of the tank fit into this guide rail device. Above the area and centered, they mounted a bomb shackle to hold the inserted tank by its hooks.

They installed pumps and lines to bring the new store of auxiliary fuel to the main integral wing self-sealing tanks. The auxiliary tank would be the first to empty and once empty, discarded.

In spite of time-constrained working conditions, the planes from the Third and the 345th Groups were ready for the mission to Wewak, scheduled for August 17, providing another great example of field modification under time and material pressures. The airmen were ready as well.

At our standard 140 gallon-per-hour burn, Kenney had increased our range, giving us two additional hours of flying time. With that tank we could take on the more distant targets that the Japanese had anticipated being safely out of B-25 territory. Thus evolved the deadliest bomber in the Southwest Pacific. It provided the type of offense that met all the requirements of the time and the place. Brought to fruition was Chief of the Army Air Corps General Hap Arnold's dictum: The number one job of an air force is bombardment. We must have the long-range bombers which can hit the enemy before he hits us. The best defense is attack. Now, we had an awesome long range attack weapon and Wewak was vulnerable.

Although Dobodura could now serve as an ideal base for striking targets around the Huon Gulf, on New Britain and in the Bismarck Sea beyond, a direct flight route from this new base to the Wewak targets took us over the active Japanese airfields at Salamaua, Lae and Madang on the northern coast. Those bases could not only provide enemy air opposition but would have been able to pass on a warning of our approach, alerting our objective.

So we decided to stage this first major raid against Wewak through the Seven-Mile airbase at Jackson near Port Moresby, refuel and proceed northwest on an inland route paralleling the south side of the Owen Stanley Range. Not flying near enemy airstrips. No hint of our intended destination.

Our Third Attack Group commander, Colonel D. P. Hall, led the mission, one of his final missions before rotating home. Two and a half hours into it, some 40 or 50 miles from the target, he descended to tree-top level. Hugging the hills, he rose a little over the coconut trees to check his position for a straight run on Borum, the first targeted airstrip at Wewak.

He couldn't believe his eyes. Sixty Japanese planes lined each side of the Borum strip, wing tip to wing tip. Maintenance crews in and out of vehicles were running around. Ground crews were perched on engine work stands. Incredible.

There had been no warning. The enemy never suspected the development of this new B-25 range and considered their expanding bases well out of danger,

From left to right: Capt. Fitch, Lt. Jones, Capt. Ellis, Lt. Helbreigel, Maj. Henebry, Capt. Cline, Lt. Bersch, and Lt. Hicks

protected primarily by distance. Any outlying observers or patrol planes either didn't exist or didn't have time to communicate with the Wewak headquarters and airstrips. Radar came later to Wewak but Hall's tree top approach was too low to be detected anyway. Colonel Hall had accomplished the most valuable offensive maneuver—a surprise attack.

Even our fighter cover held back, coming on a few minutes after our strike to avoid their presence serving as an alert. The enemy did not know Wewak was under attack until DP's fire began ripping up the strip with his specialized 23-pound parafrags—the wicked never-used parachute fragmentation bombs that General Kenney invented for another war.

Long before our entrance into World War II, General Kenney had developed the parafrag. It was a mean weapon designed to throw lethal shrapnel fragments in a 360-degree pattern. The fuse on the parafrag was so sensitive that a blade of grass could set it off. When it hit, it exploded like a 23-pound hand grenade, doing great damage to parked airplanes and motor vehicles, wounding and killing personnel.

The parafrag was a partner in Kenney's low level air attack tactics since it was created to be dropped from a plane at minimum altitude. Fitted with a small parachute about four feet in diameter that opened on release from the bomb bay, slowing and straightening the bomb's descent, the timing gave the pilot his chance to move away from the shockwave of the explosion.

The parafrag addressed one of the initial problems of bombing from anywhere less than 100 feet: the tendency of an armed bomb to continue skipping along its predestined path after making contact with a target able to trigger the delayed fuse but unable to halt the bomb. Delayed fuse bombs, 100-pounds and up, were thus not the ideal weapons to drop from minimum altitude. Planting a bomb that size required extreme accuracy when the target was anything less than a ship, a tank or a truck. Dropped on a smaller target, the bomb better hit and it better stay put or you became your own target. While the delayed fuse did keep the released bomb from exploding immediately on impact under a low flying plane taking the plane out with the target, if the bomb didn't stay with the target, it stayed with the plane, "flying formation" for those three, four or five seconds of programmed delay until it finally blew, damaging or destroying the plane.

The parafrag was Kenney's solution for a safe, direct, predictable, exclusive delivery. The Third was the first to employ the bomb as a standard weapon. Colonel Hall made this historic delivery.

The morning of the August 17th mission, DP split his 36-strong B-25 force into four segments. Hall as overall leader had hit the first strip, Borum. Within minutes, seven squadrons hit each of three other airstrips with equal surprise and ferocity. Bomb craters pockmark the area to this day.

The strike was classically successful. Returning pilots all reported in with great enthusiasm. None of us could understand why the Japanese parked their

Third Attack Group B-25's strike Japanese airbase in New Guinea. Parafrags are dropped over the airstrip, destroying the parked aircraft and equipment.

planes so tidily wing tip to wing tip instead of dispersing them throughout the area to minimize their vulnerability. Perhaps Japanese airmen remained the assured force prepared to fight the same kind of war that had brought victories in China and Southeast Asia. Perhaps they didn't recognize that here was a different enemy with new tactics. Perhaps the Wewak bases had been set up for safe review by Japanese brass as new units came into the theater to revitalize their campaign. Don't know. But parked they were and destroy them we did.

We were never sure of the exact numbers. A high level reconnaissance photo taken from 25,000 feet five minutes before our first strike had shown 176 planes parked on the four target airstrips. Since every sitting plane hit does not burn, we were denied our primary evidence of damage. But a crippled plane may never fly again. A bomb can be fatal to a plane without hitting its fuel tank but without that fuel tank explosion, it is tough to estimate from the air overall damage to planes and ground vehicles.

A couple of freighters sat in the Wewak harbor to the right of Borum airstrip. After our initial pass on that primary target, I made a run over one of the ships. Good hunting. A sure shot. To line up for the strafing run I committed a cardinal mistake. I made a turn bellying up to a shore battery that shot us up, blowing off our ingenious spring-loaded rear doors that fortunately already had released their empty auxiliary tank.

A simple, valuable lesson about this type of aggressive aviation sunk in that day. I had had my guns on that Japanese ack-ack that was firing on me in defense of its airstrip and should have continued my run on that position. If you keep your fire on a gunner, putting some of that fifty-caliber into him, you discourage him like hell from firing back at you. I was doing that. When you take your guns off him, and I did that too, you free him to shoot. He did.

But that juicy target was sitting in the harbor distracting me. I made a run on the ship and got myself shot up a little bit, not seriously. We made it home relatively intact.

They did shoot up one of the planes before it even reached the target. An Italian fellow from New Jersey, Ralph Cheli (we Irish called him Kelly), was a commander leading his squadron's attack on Dulag, the airstrip beyond Borum. Disabled—hit hard and with his plane on fire—he kept it under control and his outfit together through strafing and bombing, then ditched in the ocean after his run. He and his crew were assumed dead from reports of the crash brought back by others in his squadron. He, as the pilot and leader of his squadron, was awarded the Congressional Medal of Honor posthumously.

But more than two years later when we finally occupied Rabaul, we recovered five American flyers who had been captured and imprisoned there. They reported, to our amazement, that Cheli had survived the August 17th crash in the sea off Wewak and had been taken prisoner. He had been interned with them at Rabaul, spending his imprisonment unloading supply ships in the harbor. Though Cheli

In preparation for decoration ceremony (left to right): Brigadier General Jimmie Crabb, Lieutenant General Ennis Whitehead, John Henebry and Major Scott Dennison, review the airmen in 1943.

Lieutenant General Ennis Whitehead enthusiastically presented medals to the airmen

had been killed finally in an Allied bomb attack on Simpson Harbor, his compatriots proudly reported he had been tough, ornery and uncooperative with his captors to the end.

Since we had no exact way of calculating the extent of the destruction of the first attack, to be sure to inflict the maximum damage we ran another mission the next day and hit Wewak again. I was tapped to lead my squadron.

I was ready. I had feared the unknown in the early days of the war. I had made some mistakes that I never repeated. I had survived. Throughout that original raid against Wewak I had experienced the most fear I have ever known. But my solid combat experience had taught me well.

Fear is a part of war. Although courage seems to show no fear, it really only suppresses fear. We had our fearful pilots. Those who lost their guts, reporting engine problems before missions. Pilots who reported physical problems that would send them temporarily to Australia or permanently home. Officers who would vomit in the mess before a mission. I would take such men in my command up and fly with them to work out their fears. I made them fly. Reassured them. Or I would shoot them back to headquarters to take up other jobs. Most recovered from their fears. Most would fly the missions assigned to them.

Still, this Wewak attack scared me because the mission took us farther than we had ever flown in our air battle careers. But day one of the mission had been so successful that in spite of the damage to my plane my confidence soared and by the second day when I led the clean-up attack, I was more sure of my own abilities and the capabilities of our weapons, our squadron and General Kenney's attack aviation theories.

Though my fear may have subsided, reason to fear remained. We met increased ground fire the second day. The Japanese were more alert, having lost not only planes in the previous day's strike but any sense of security they might have had, believing they were beyond our range.

When the reports reached the top, Generals MacArthur and Kenney were truly elated. Their congratulatory communications reflected their keen awareness of this two-day mission's impact on MacArthur's strategic plans. Neutralizing Wewak was a significant step in the Allied thrust toward the Philippines. It broke the back of the Japanese hold on the Southwest Pacific.

Again the success of the B-25s conversion to a long range minimum altitude strafer and bomber had exceeded even General Kenney's expectations. Under his design, the Mitchell had come a long way from the twin-engine, twin-turret, light attack bomber that originally had appeared in 1939.

And beyond MacArthur and Kenney were the Pentagon, Wright Field and North American Aviation, who eventually produced our Australian conversion of their Mitchell bomber at the Inglewood, California factory. Kenney then could and would put his field crews to other imaginative uses.

11

"Steak and Eggs" and "Fat Cat"

THE "Good Life" on Papua New Guinea was a primitive, substandard existence. The island offered nothing that resembled home, not a desirable place to be in the 1940s. Minimal extravagances made memories. An air mattress, a folding cot and a mosquito net were the symbols of luxury. No grocery stores. Rather, food produced locally, sold in native markets for consumption by the indigenous people. No whiskey rations, not until the latter part of 1943 when finally two ounces were allowed after a debriefing. No diversions. No escape. We depended equally on each other and Uncle Sam to supply us with everything considered essential to winning a war. We expected and received little more. We were uncomfortable, deprived, restricted, stressed and dislocated. Fertile ground for American ingenuity.

If you are hungry enough, bully beef, dehydrated potatoes, canned milk and canned peaches taste good. We wouldn't starve. In addition, we had the field Army with its amazing feeding organization. Regardless of who was the head officer, soon emerged the guy who really ran the unit, the mess sergeant, usually a master sergeant. He knew everyone who worked for and around him—their assignments, their connections, their scopes of responsibility. Rarely, probably never, a gourmet chef, he needed only to boil water, heat up the grease for frying, bake some gut-filling concoctions. He never had the "makin's" to go beyond that.

He served us all, equally, no small job. In the field, moving forward base to base, the officers and enlisted men alike ate from the same mess sergeant's kitchen. Separate tents, but the same dull food.

Cleanliness was his primary responsibility. Boiling water and a scrub brush were his essential tools. In the tropics food poisoning was always a threat. The flight surgeon was the great overseer assuring that the mess sergeant kept his kingdom clean and that everyone beyond the kitchen, officers and enlisted men alike, cleaned their personal mess kits in boiling water. The pots, pans and utensils gleamed. The food was lackluster.

We were well into the war before food refrigerators caught up with us. Canned food, packaged in the States, had long been the basis of our meals. Australia supplemented the staples with some occasional meat and potatoes. Without refrigeration, food was not left standing. No snacking on leftovers. Cans were opened and their contents consumed or discarded immediately. Mess was clean, uncontaminated and uninspired.

Month after month of this fare had been hard on the Eighty-Ninth, the first squadron to move to New Guinea and the first to have a full complement of airplanes—original A-20s brought over in 1942 from Savannah, modified in Australia.

It was the Eighty-Ninth who countered the Japanese assault on the Owen Stanley's Kokoda Trail in the enemy effort to capture Port Moresby. A-20s spent a lot of time in the air locating and strafing the Japanese in support of the Australian ground forces defending the mountain-top entry to southern New Guinea.

During all of this hard flying, enemy fire hit plane number 40166, one of the Eighty-Ninth's A-20s, forcing it to land at nearby Seven-Mile airstrip. The landing was successful under the circumstances. The main gear touched down, the A-20 slowed and tipped forward. The crew waited for the nose wheel to hit and complete the ground roll. The nose wheel was shot up as the enemy fire had knocked it out so the plane continued tipping, landing like a butterfly with sore feet. Though the underside of the nose section was damaged extensively, Lieutenant Bill Ford and his rear gunner were unhurt and the fuselage was intact.

The Eighth Service Group at Seven-Mile stripped away all usable parts, registering them in supply. The relatively undamaged fuselage was considered valueless and relegated to the junk pile. The military prided itself in its ability to keep track of what it owns and what it pitches. A captain could get defrocked if a rifle were missing.

For the men of the Eighty-Ninth squadron life had been relatively bland. Many of them continually wondered how they could get at the well-remembered supplies of beer and fresh food back in Australia having no conceivable civil nor military communication nor delivery system in place, not by land, sea nor air.

Soon creative minds mulled the bright idea of developing a private transport service. Looking at Ford's 40166 over at Seven-Mile and all the A-20s at Three-Mile crippled by enemy fire, ground damage or wanting spare parts, these dreamers saw usable parts in planes that can't fly gathered together into one good flying machine. Cannibalizing they called it.

"Little Hellion," A-20 number 40166, after landing at Seven-Mile Airstrip

A couple of weeks later one of the Eighty-Ninth linemen at Three-Mile, trying to move A-20A number 39724, with a Cletrac fastened to the nose wheel, got a little rough and pulled the strut, nose wheel and all, off the plane. The nose dropped to the ground causing more damage to the fuselage than Bill Ford had done during his landing over at Seven-Mile.

The Eighty-Ninth Squadron engineering officer, Major John R. "Robbie" Robinson, had been in charge of all aircraft maintenance since he had come over from Savannah in January 1942. He knew his A-20s like a book, and he knew all the men in the area who had worked on them.

His original plan was to repair 39724, smoothing out its twisted nose and wrinkled fuselage. A tough job. His men rigged up some empty fuel drums and with aircraft jacks hoisted the A20 up on the drums.

Such a challenge was enough to stimulate Robbie's imagination. The time to make dreams a reality was now. He remembered 40166 on the junk pile at Seven-Mile and envisioned the integration of the best of those two wrecks. His service group's mechanical know-how plus just enough larceny in the blood could and would produce something worthwhile.

He gained the confidence of Colonel Shaw, commander of the neighboring Eighth Service Group at Seven-Mile, and before many people sensed the activity, he had the stripped, discarded fuselage on a flatbed on its way to Three-Mile, together with two new purloined Pratt & Whitney engines, two new propellers and other parts and equipment necessary for the resuscitation.

The something useful of Robbie's imagination would be a noble stripped down ex-warbird incidentally capable of carrying fresh food and maybe some beer up from Australia to the Eighty-Ninth Squadron stuck at Three-Mile fighting a difficult war.

Without fanfare Robbie started on the job of rebuilding the A-20. Others in the Eighty-Ninth began to see its worthwhile objectives. Help became abundant. The whole quiet project became a subtle morale builder.

As it built morale, it used up a lot of discomforting spare time, time normally spent fantasizing other times in other places. Eventually it became a major competition among all the experts in the squadron to see who could contribute the most toward the rebirth of the plane. The whole of the United States was represented. Tex Sevcik, Kip Hawkins of New Hampshire, John Dugan of Pennsylvania, Joe Schramm from New England. Johnnie Leonard, Joe Cline, Parrott, Zuker, Ruddell, Mack Cunningham, Whitehouse and Meister and, for that matter, almost everyone in the squadron wanted to and did help. To name everyone who pitched in to put that A-20 in the air would be to publish the squadron roster.

Finally came the day to christen "The Steak and Egg Special." The squadron commander, the squadron operations officer and Colonel D. P. Hall decorously were not present for this illicit launch but Lieutenant Charles Brown gave a short speech and Lieutenant Ocal Jones christened the A-20 with an egg-cracking ceremony. Where the fresh egg came from remains a mystery. It would be the first flying cannibal in New Guinea.

The new freighter flew and after a few flights south to the mainland, the olive drab paint was stripped off and a bright new silver finish was waxed and polished into its surface. A shortened name, simply "Steak and Eggs," still pronounced with an Australian twist ("Styk 'n Aigs"), was painted back on the nose.

For nearly a year the rejuvenated bird made overnight flights south to the lean markets of Australia and back to the bon vivants of the Eighty-Ninth with its party loads of steak, eggs, beer and platters of the Andrews sisters, Tommy Dorsey, Duke Ellington and Jo Stafford.

The happy era ended in bad weather when "Steak and Eggs," flown by Lieutenant Vukelic, made its last landing, forced but with no injuries, onto a reef in the Coral Sea off Townsville. It rests there still.

During that year cannibalization became a normal Air Force solution in the jungle, with nothing considered beyond the reach of a combat plane's mechanics. We were aggressively attacking Japanese shipping and air installations now. Our planes were returning from battle damaged, malfunctioning or wearing out. War-weary aircraft was fixed pronto or it was vulnerable. Though the flow of replacement aircraft and parts was steady, what was arriving was not always the right piece at the right place at the right time. When healthier planes

"Steak and Eggs" ready to fly

with savvy crews needed parts to put them back in the air and the particular needed replacement part was not available on base, a quick fix for a resourceful crew chief was often a quick switch with a grounded or partially grounded aircraft. Gradually a plane would be totally stripped of all that was useful, sacrificed to keep others flying.

Our base had moved north over the Owen Stanley Range and we were exposed to a lot of combat after the Bismarck Sea victory in March. Increased damage was inevitable so when three of our beat-up B-25's were consigned to the heap, they became ripe pickin's for the cannibals. Had we been based closer to supply lines, parts would have been available and legitimate repairs would have been made. The three would have met a more honorable end. At Dobodura, a mountain and a sea away from Australia, such were not the conditions.

It happened in the best of airdromes. It happened in the Ninetieth in 1943 when the three ailing B-25s were cannibalized to come up with one complete flyable aircraft. "Fat Cat." A plane minus 3,000-pounds of guns and munitions, no ammunition feed racks, its bomb bay welded shut, divested of all excess equipment needed for combat flying—even the olive drab paint was removed. A plane without identification. A plane whose only purpose was to fly south and return with the products of a civilized society.

The idea was nurtured on the success of "Steak and Eggs" created the year before at Port Moresby.

"Fat Cat" also was a squadron team effort—sheet metal workers, instrument specialists, engine geniuses. Master Sergeant John B. Chesson was a major spark plug. Murry Orvin specializing in crew chiefing airplanes. Sergeants Meredith Bryant and Bill Hackett urging the men on. I was Squadron Commander and cooperatively turned a blind eye. The resulting "Fat Cat" became the only stripped-down hot rod B-25 in the Pacific theater.

"Fat Cat" at christening ceremony with some of the airmen
who built the plane from three wrecked B-25 airplanes.

"Fat Cat" was lightweight, its most exciting and useful characteristic. The first time I started the engines it became apparent that the plane was hot. I quickly and heavily applied the brakes to restrain it from taxiing out of control. On the first take-off the right propeller ran away because of a prop governor malfunction. Even after I shut the engine down and feathered the prop, I climbed straight out to 800 feet, half circled to 180 degrees and landed on our one runway. So light, "Fat Cat" had flown back on its one engine like a homesick angel.

The Ninetieth helped retake Lae, Salamaua and Nadzab. Concurrent with those victories "Fat Cat" was transporting untallied quantities of beer and sausage to the men of Dobodura. It brought men south a dozen or so at a time to shake the jungle out of their jump suits and back again to take up the fight. It established a fine reputation logging quite a few jaunts down to Australia—before its existence inevitably came to the attention of the Fifth Bomber Command.

Then, with lightening confiscation orders, it was no more.

The Leapfrog Classic

SOME evening coastal traffic reported along the underside of the Japanese-held island of New Britain kept us in the air. The 300 mile-long island sat 150 to 200 miles north and east of our base at Dobodura, New Guinea. Rabaul provided fortification on its east. On the west a lesser, yet effective, base at Cape Gloucester protected this strategic plot of land.

We were looking for "targets of opportunity" related to New Britain, beginning at the airfield at Gasmata, north across the Solomon Sea, and swinging west and up to Cape Gloucester.

Colonel D. P. Hall, our Group Commander, had put together five flights of B-25s, three planes each, to hunt the area. Each of the three-plane formations was to fly in trail at a couple hundred feet altitude, a good coast-searching altitude, with the lead formation descending to work over whatever caught the lead pilot's eye.

The following flight was then to leapfrog the flight in action and continue as lead along the coast to find its next "target of opportunity."

I was leading Captains Howe and MacLellan in the third flight. D. P. had spotted some activity and had taken his formation down to work it over. Howe, MacLellan and I were now second in line, proceeding westward. The new lead flight picked out a target and swooped down on it.

Now my third flight had leapfrogged into the lead. We proceeded westward and followed the coast as it turned north around Mount Tangi. As we neared the Cape Gloucester airstrip I saw up high—at least at 10,000 feet—a number of single engine fighters circling. Japanese.

The sight was disquieting, primarily because we were flying without fighter cover that day. We often flew missions without cover, as P-38s were scarce. Not many had been assigned to the theater at this point in the Pacific war. The inventory was increasing but none were with us flying to New Britain.

The enemy fighter planes were hovering in a lufbery circle, a defensive tactic originally created by French and American airmen in World War I, where fighters circle at the same altitude protecting each other to preclude an attacking enemy fighter penetrating the pattern. An intruder does so at the risk of exposing his rear to fire.

A lufbery circle usually indicates a target worth protecting. And sure enough, there in front of us about three miles off the coast, were two large destroyers, commonly used by the enemy to run supplies and personnel.

As "targets of opportunity" go, this was a dream. Scouting missions didn't often catch enemy destroyers in open water at sea. Here below us were not one, but two.

As the current lead, I started my descent from about 200 feet above the coast line to make a run on the nearest of the two destroyers. As an appetizer, flying right into my line of attack, was a twin engine Japanese transport plane making a left turn for an approach to the Cape Gloucester airstrip, intent on resupplying or evacuating the base.

I turned slightly to make a pass at it, getting in close enough to aim two good bursts into his right engine. It started burning and, according to my top gunner, the plane crashed in flames on the airstrip.

Meanwhile, the Japanese fighters kept their altitude. They stayed in good surveillance position at 10,000 feet, able to dive out of danger should U.S. fighter cover attack, which they assumed would be the scenario. To fly at an altitude underneath the expected enemy fighters would put their planes in jeopardy.

Unobstructed then, I continued my descent to wave-top altitude, lining up for my strafing bomb run.

Howe and MacLellan, flying left and right wing positions, pulled in nice and tight. The air was clear and bright with little wind—perfect air for tight, minimum altitude flying. I was flanked by the best. With practiced ease, Howe and MacLellan could hold their wing positions, fire forward and drop a bomb load with fingers to spare. Compared to their complicated jobs, my responsibility to lead the formation was easy. I needed only to take my flight to the right place at the right time.

This place and time started heating up. Both destroyers started firing at us. Their heavy guns were making a few water spouts but nothing at first was coming really close. Howe, MacLellan and I were making a 90 degree broadside pass, setting up the best approach for our bombs. However, we were also setting ourselves up as ideal targets for their gunners.

So we proceeded toward the destroyer, flying as low as we could fly, so low we were probably leaving a wake in the water. The destroyers' lighter guns began to fire. It could have been a blinking Christmas tree before us, the fire was so rapid and extensive.

As a defensive move, I pulled my nose up slightly to stretch the mile range of my eight forward firing machine guns, lobbing my fire on their decks.

Our fire wouldn't sink a man-o'-war but I knew sure as hell we could cause a lot of confusion with all the stuff the three of us with our 24 fifty-calibers were throwing at them. I doubt that a fifty-caliber even could pierce the armor surrounding the guns on deck. But all that splattering surely made those seamen duck. And may have wiped out a few.

An effective move. They stopped firing. The blinking lights darkened. The maneuver had worked previously for Larner against the cruiser in the Bismarck Sea and it worked for us. None of our three planes was hit.

I dropped two delayed fuse 500-pound bombs into the side of one of the ships. The gunner reported two solid hits as we pulled up to clear the mast and descended back down to sea level as a defensive move.

By now all five flights were involved in the attack, the original two having caught up with us. I made a 180 degree turn for another run on the ship from the other side. It was a much quieter target. I hit him again with a 500-pounder.

Half of that ship still sticks up out of the waters off Cape Gloucester. When the captain realized his ship was sinking, he ran it aground on a reef to keep it from going under. And there it stays.

The Japanese fighters remained at 10,000 feet prepared to take on our non-existent cover fighters. Throughout all our days of battle with Japanese pilots, they continued to be hesitant to sacrifice their altitude to come down to engage us until they were sure no fighter cover was protecting our runs. In this battle, by the time they realized we were flying uncovered and made a conscientious effort to pursue us, the damage had been complete—a transport aircraft downed and two destroyers sunk. We headed home before they entered the air we had claimed.

The 75 Millimeter Cannon

WE were flirting with the French 75.

Fifty-caliber Browning machine guns had been the staple since we had arrived in the Southwest Pacific. Our low level strafing B-25s were fully loaded with eight firing forward, each armed with 400 rounds of ammunition. The squadron of A-20s carried six each. Rear power turrets carried an additional two as protection against fighter aircraft attacks.

Even with that, we always wanted more firepower. We were well into the war now fighting heavily fortified concentrated targets. Japanese pilots were fighting with a fury, feeling that each held the key to the destiny of his homeland. Our low flying missions had taken on a dimension beyond destroying the objective. Now we were neutralizing the enemy's withering ground fire.

The airmen's favorite speculation was how and where to mount more guns. We couldn't find an answer in machine guns. Adding more fifties was not easy to do on our already bomb-laden, gun-laden planes. Maybe 20 millimeter guns . . .

Our neighbors, the Royal Australian Air Force Thirtieth Squadron, flew Beaufighters equipped with four 20 millimeter cannons and were shooting a good war. But Beaufighters carried no bomb load. Nevertheless we became interested in that gun as a way to increase our potency and quiet down enemy defenses.

The RAAF planes and their guns were being made in England. We had heard of some American-made 20 millimeters around on European theater Air Corps planes. We never saw any. We never got any. The official line was that the 20 millimeter gun was not as reliable as were our fifty-calibers—and that its ammunition was not as readily available.

Certainly the precision needed to engineer and install added guns would be difficult now that we had moved to our jungle base north and west, farther away from our most logical and tested modification facility in Australia. So speculation eventually quieted down and we settled in again with our fifty-caliber equipment. It continued proving itself through many missions. It must have been good. We were firing enough of it.

July 1943, along comes Pappy Gunn unveiling his newest B-25 sporting a forward-firing 75 millimeter cannon—of the same style as the popular WWI French 75. Some scuttlebutt about a cannon-equipped B-25 had preceded Pappy's arrival. We dismissed it as farfetched until that bright day when Pappy grandly landed at the Dobodura airstrip.

In Pappy's version, the cannon was mounted in the tunnel that leads to the bombardier compartment in the plane nose. The breech and reserve shells were in the navigator compartment behind the pilot where the engineer or "cannoneer" threw shells into it by hand, one at a time.

After the pilot fired the first shell from a button finger switch on his control wheel—much like the machine gun button we were used to—the cannon breach opened, ejecting the empty shell casing into the navigator compartment. The cannoneer threw another shell into the breach. it closed and automatically armed the shell. When the cannon was ready to fire, the cannoneer whacked the pilot on the back to indicate the 75 had been loaded and ready for his trigger finger.

The cannoneer preset each shell to explode at a predetermined range—seconds, or fractions thereof—or to explode on contact. The pilot's decision. The pilot was taking his sighting two miles off the target at a couple hundred feet altitude, well beyond the range of fifty-caliber guns.

It was a pilot toy. It added a new dimension to flying. Once he released the projectile, a pilot with little else to do in his cockpit could follow it in flight. It left no tracer, but highly visible was a three inch circle, like a baseball moving straight ahead at a high rate of speed. The shell arched downward after a few hundred yards of flat flying as gravity came into play. The trajectory was predictable but accuracy in placing the explosion initially took some practice.

A special sight was soon devised to improve the pilot ability to aim accurately, to determine range, speed and trajectory.

In principal, the design was sound, save for one fault: The plane had to be flying high enough, straight and level to see the target and take advantage of the cannon range. We could never induce the enemy to cooperate, to stop the war momentarily while the pilot arranged all the prerequisites for fulfillment of the weapon capabilities.

The Third tested this first installation of the 75 and we were furnished with some very sound, factual information before we took it into combat against live targets. An undercurrent of stories floated aplenty around about the 75 millimeter installation before it made its appearance at Dobodura. It was "known" to jar the airframe to pieces. The force of it "stopped planes in mid-air." Crew members' "ear drums broke." Latrine-based scuttlebutt.

In actuality, Pappy's was a very good installation, well engineered. Good

North American Aviation Field Rep. Jack Fox standing in front of "Lil' Fox,"
with the 75 millimeter cannon mounted in the nose of this B-25.

recoil mechanism. We flew and fired with no airframe disintegration, one function not interfering with the other. A micro-second thud was its only accompanying noise, not loud, not extreme. Eardrums were not damaged. The steady B-25 engine noise caused more ear damage than could any repercussions from cannon fire—as my present impaired state of hearing will attest.

The installation had been completed at the North American B-25 factory at Inglewood California under Pappy's very critical eye. He was there, he advised everyone, "to get those knuckleheads straightened out." It was Pappy's chalk drawings on the plane's exterior, according to Pappy, that guided "all those smart-ass engineers" through this very exacting placement of our 75 millimeter cannon.

All four of our squadron commanders and most of the Third pilots took advantage of the opportunity either to fly and fire the 75 or observe it in action. After frequent and serious exchanges of opinions among our highly experienced pilots and combat crews we, and especially I, had to decide for or against changing our way of doing business and accepting the conversion to the 75 millimeter or continuing our proven tactics with our fifty-caliber machine guns.

These were my pilots and my planes. I was Group Commander now and was eager to welcome new artillery, especially a touted weapon such as the 75 looked to be. I first flew the plane on several practice missions out of Dobodura, firing the cannon. Then I flew it against the Wewak airstrips in two combat missions.

All that activity. All that power. The challenge was fun at first and provided diversion during our unrelenting war. But introducing a new weapon in the midst of battle is complicated. While the added fire power was inviting, this weapon introduced unexpected problems that had to be overcome as I experienced them surfacing in the midst of battle.

The 75 cannon was not ultimate weaponry. All that slow, primitive back-thumping became objectionable. We missed the ease of our faithful fifty-calibers that the cannon had replaced.

Back at headquarters, the Fifth Air Force seemed to have fallen in love with the plane-mounted cannon. The Port Moresby brass in the late summer of 1943 was proposing we re-equip all aircraft in our three squadrons.

After the cannon had its extensive trials I said no, not in my planes. Not for my men. Not enough versatility. Certainly too slow to load. In my pass over Borum I got off only one round. I witnessed only a few B-25 crews getting off at most two rounds on a single pass. Not enough destruction the first time over. Making a second pass over a well-defended target such as Borum was not advised; it can shorten your life. Gone was the surprise factor of an attacking plane making its initial approach and pass over. That one round released does not justify the accompanying exposure to enemy fire. If that one shot misses, you don't leave much damage in your wake or suppress much ground fire and second chances aren't often offered. Lost is the whole purpose of exposing your low flying aircraft to enemy defenses.

And further, the range of the 75 required too much altitude to sight, just as we were becoming specialists as low altitude strafers in surprise approaches to our jungle and harbor targets. We were attackers. Our greatest effectiveness was when we surprised and overwhelmed the enemy. Surprise gave us our ultimate protection, minimum exposure to enemy fire, along with the best chance at shooting and bombing accuracy.

We compared the one-shot cannon to the capability of our potent fifty-caliber machine guns. Its 400 rounds for each of eight guns firing repeatedly through a target and its defenses afforded us the ability to not only suppress enemy fire but place our bomb loads accurately in the target area.

Hand-loaded weapons weren't that threatening. The rate of fire of the 75 millimeter was too restrictive against a well-defended target. It couldn't suppress enemy fire. Our B-25s were too exposed for too few rounds fired.

An isolated target, weakly defended, a lone building or a single vehicle provided great shooting with the 75. That was not the stuff we were in the skies for. We were going after heavily guarded Japanese airfields and men-o'-war. In my Southwest Pacific experience, no strike on a man-o'-war in harbor or at sea employed the 75 millimeter cannon. The stakes were too high.

Later on as the war progressed northward, more lethal models of the B-25H did appear with not only the 75 millimeter installed but with as many as twelve fifty-calibers supporting it and a 3,000-pound bomb capacity. That made more sense to those of us moving that bomb line toward Japan.

Now, though, we continued depending on our machine guns, factory rated at firing 1,100 rounds per minute. We were actually realizing about nine hundred. Even cutting back to 900 rounds per minute still did a lot of damage and offered us a lot of protection. By not setting the rate of fire controls too high and backing down a little, the guns were more reliable. We weren't melting metal. We were jamming less. It was better having all eight guns firing at a reduced rate than having only five or six, or often less, able to keep the 1,100 rate.

Hot barrels were a vital concern. Continuous fire at a rapid rate quickly heated the barrels to such a high temperature that the direction of fire became uncontrollable. The bullets tumbled in any direction—right, left, up or down, distorting a compact field of fire.

Or, worse yet, the guns jammed and stopped firing altogether. We paced our fire to avoid these troubles.

From a distance, up to a mile from a chosen target, our best tactic was a series of short bursts to get some fire onto the objective, conserving the barrels and the ammunition until we closed in. Then we increased the rate of fire safely while maintaining accuracy.

The demand for perfection in each gun and every shell was merciless. The

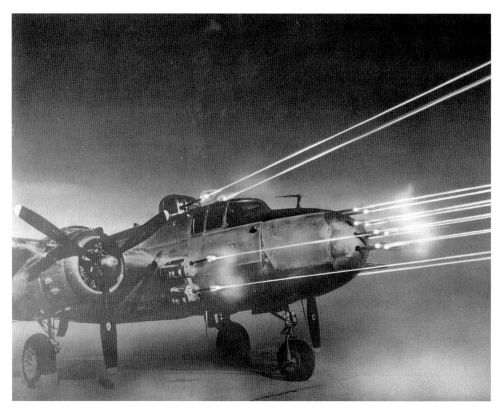
Photo displays the potential fire power of the B-25

slightest imperfection would make the combination of the two worthless—
intolerable in the many unrelenting situations we found ourselves.

Added to the zero tolerances in manufacture was the need to accommodate for
the differing rates of expansion and contraction in the various metals brought on
by the extreme temperatures of our equatorial war zone. That too was built in. We
had very few, if any, gun failures due to engineering or manufacturing mistakes.

Great credit is due to the U.S. Army Ordnance Department which oversaw the
government and civilian manufacturers and material suppliers who themselves were
coping with the department-particular demands in addition to general wartime
demands and material shortages. This was a production phenomenon.

The amazing statistic of World War II was the amount of fifty-caliber
ammunition that was produced and the number of fifty-caliber machine guns
that were manufactured for our aircraft. According to Lieutenant Colonel Michael
Wolfert of the office of the Air Force Chief of Staff at Air Force Headquarters
researching Army records, Americans produced one and a half million fifty-
caliber machine guns for aircraft and—a number that few people, including
me, could fathom—more than ten billion rounds of fifty-caliber ammunition.

These figures are only one small, but vital, example of the productivity of the once-sleeping giant. Our armed aircraft was a big item, but all the other supporting equipment such as trucks, shops, equipment and supplies were the result of our massive, intricate, dependable national effort. Our overwhelming industrial strength, kicked into high gear December 7, 1941, assured our ultimate victory from day one. And no wonder. When the supply organization backing up the assault forces instantaneously brought all our stuff ashore onto island after island, there was little room left for an enemy to function.

Rabaul

HEAD northwest, move up St. George's Channel, go past the Cape Gazelle lighthouse point, past the South Daughter Volcano. Beyond the highest point of The Mother ahead, make a left turn to slip between The Mother and North Daughter. Continue southwest.

What a sight you'll see.

The town of Rabaul on the northeastern tip of New Britain commands the magnificent Simpson Harbor between the Bismarck and Solomon Seas. Because Simpson Harbor is one of the world's most protective natural sea shelters, in February 1942, two months after the Japanese attacked Pearl Harbor, their military occupied this strategic naval anchorage, developing it into the strongest enemy base in the Southwest Pacific Area.

From this command post at Rabaul the Japanese supported an aggressive downward thrust of its army, navy and air forces through the South Pacific toward New Guinea and Australia. While some factions of the Japanese command wanted to occupy the island and the mainland, the Coral Sea rebuff in the spring of 1942 and a subsequent inability to establish a base at Port Moresby on the southern coast of New Guinea prompted more practical Japanese minds to settle on the lesser goal of merely isolating Australia behind a string of conquered islands lacing up to China.

In Japanese hands, Rabaul developed four major airfields—Lukunai, Rapopo, Vunakanau and Tobera—extensive army garrisons housing 100,000 infantrymen and naval support facilities. The bulging munitions warehouses, normally storing a six-month inventory of goods and materiel, allowed the enemy to move west across Indonesia and up into Burma in a continuing quest for oil, rubber, food and land. A heavy concentration of more than 350 anti-aircraft weapons, and later radar capable of giving a 30 to 60 minute advance attack warning, protected it.

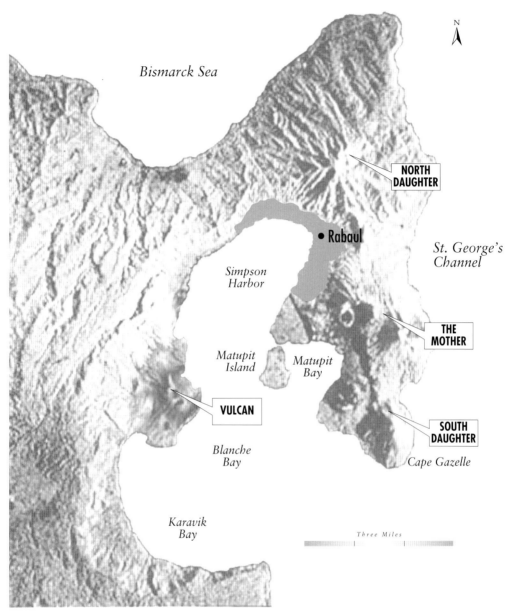

N

Bismarck Sea

NORTH DAUGHTER

• Rabaul

St. George's Channel

Simpson Harbor

THE MOTHER

Matupit Island

Matupit Bay

VULCAN

SOUTH DAUGHTER

Blanche Bay

Cape Gazelle

Karavik Bay

Three Miles

Topographic view of Rabaul with volcano locations:
North Daughter, The Mother, South Daughter, and Vulcan

Rabaul became a prime target for U.S. air power. At first we hit with sporadic nighttime and high altitude attacks. But as both our bomber and P-38 fighter cover gained strength, speed and range, heavy aircraft attacks on the harbor area increased. Japanese Admiral Isoroku Yamamoto's feared "sleeping giant" was directing its roar at Rabaul.

By the fall of 1943, Japanese naval air strength out of Rabaul had become formidable. But our fire power and experience had also improved. We were

General Kenney looking at a diorama of Rabaul, *Fortune* magazine, September 1943

increasing our air strikes not only against Rabaul but against other lesser but necessary Japanese air bases in the Southwest Pacific, including Wewak and Lae up the north coast of New Guinea, Cape Gloucester on the nearer New Britain coast and the Admiralty Islands, all protected by the Japanese air forces.

Because the heavies—B-17s and B-24s—were exposed to a finely developed enemy fighter aircraft defense when they attacked Japanese airfields from high

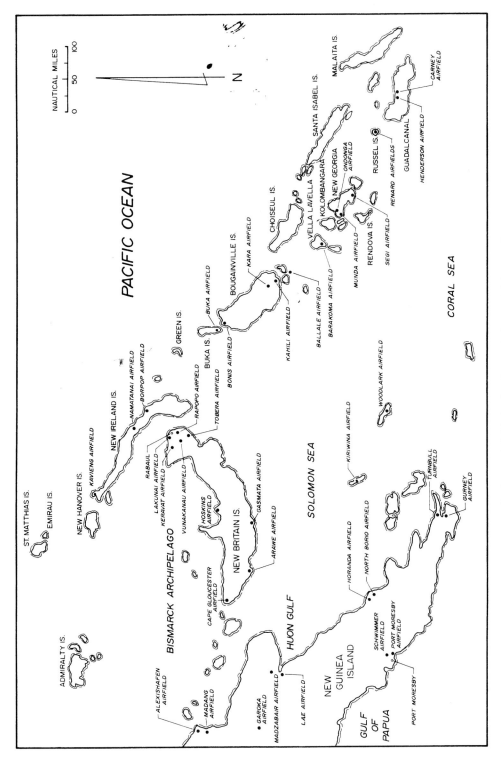

Location of military airfields in the Bismarck Sea and Solomon Sea area

111

altitude, these bombers struck in coordination with minimum altitude B-25 attacks. The basic mission to this point in the war had been to intercept and destroy Japanese fighters returning to base.

Our B-25s did more. We intercepted fighters on the ground, parked and taxiing, taking off and landing. We strafed them with fifty-caliber machine guns and bombed them with 23-pound parafrag bombs. Our attacks were devastating.

The Rabaul airstrips were spread around the harbor. We hit Vunakanau the end of August. We hit nearby Rapopo a month later. The final concentrated effort to neutralize enemy power at Rabaul began October 12. On our strikes, flying at tree top level toward the airstrips, we could see ships in the harbor, sitting at anchor. Juicy, off-limit targets. Top priority for us then remained the destruction of the enemy air capability.

Lee Van Atta and John Henebry after the October 12 raid on the airfields at Rabaul. The story on the following page was filed by Van Atta, who rode along in "Notre Dame De Victoire" during the attack.

EYEWITNESS STORY OF RABAUL SMASH

By LEE VAN ATTA

International News Service

ABOARD AN AMERICAN MITCHELL BOMBER EN ROUTE FROM RABAUL, Oct. 12.—(Delayed.)—Rabaul, key Jap bombardment base in the Southwest Pacific, was devastated today by a mighty Allied air assault, rivaling the enemy's Pearl Harbor raid.

The smoking, flaming ruins of the bombardment base seared an unforgettable, crimson impression into our minds as we hurtled our way off the target.

Caught apparently with only the briefest warning, the Rapopo Airdrome—nesting ground for Nippon's Western Pacific heavy aircraft strength—learned in all its devastating intensity the power of an American warplane attack.

TOWERS OF FIRE

Even as our forward guns began cutting a swath across Rapopo, other strafing Mitchell bombers could be seen racing against Vunakanau Airdrome. Seconds later, the scene was etched with billowing clouds of black smoke and towers of fires.

To coin a word, Rabaul was "Wewakized." The impossible has been done again—and with accomplishment of the impossible, months of planning and preparations and hours of tense anticipation have come to an end.

This correspondent rode with Maj. John (Jock) Henebry, of Plainfield Hills, Ill., veteran of 80 combat missions; Co-Pilot Lt. Edward Murphy, of Oak Park, Ill., and Navigator Lt. Abraham Soffer, of Brandford, Conn. Our deadly bomber was appropriately enough named "Notre Dame de Victore"—our lady of victory.

FIRST PROTECTED RAID

In formations spread thousands of yards across the skies with Lockheed Lightnings keeping an eternal, welcome vigilance as far as the eye could see, we roared from our advanced striking base just after dawn. For hundreds of miles, never climbing more than 60 feet above the waterline and maintaining absolutely unbroken radio silence, we sped toward the target.

It was the first time in the history of the Pacific warfare that escorted assault and bombardment units had been sent to penetrate the Japs' fortress-like ack-ack defenses around Rabaul.

By mid-morning we were over the ranges protecting Rapopo and Vunakanau from the east. The Vunakanau force and its escorting fighters swung sharply to the left while Lt. Col. Don Hall, of Corpus Christi, Tex., hero of the first Wewak raid, attacked with the second of three powerful elements comprising the Rapopo force.

We struck in split formation of three, each echelon sweeping across the airdrome and dispersal bays in beautiful waves. From a vantage point behind Henebry, bombs and machine-gun fire from Hall's lead ship could be seen pummeling down on the airdrome installations; in seconds the whole path in front of us was a holocaust of air fire, ground fire and bomb explosions.

A little later, Henebry opened his guns in a series of ear-shattering salvoes aimed at annihilating secondary antiaircraft batteries.

On our left Capt. Richard Ellis, of Laureldel, La., who similarly distinguished himself at Wewak, was swaying his fire between a Jap medium bomber attempting to scramble off the 'drome and covering bursts for his wingmen.

On the right, Lt. Charles Howe, of Ventura, Cal., piloting "Here's How," was converging his fire on the western dispersal bays with noteworthy results.

Three ships abreast we skidded into the target at the Mitchells' usually difficult-to-believe speed. Our bombs dropped among a cluster of 13 parked aircraft, while our weaving machine gunfire made a Fourth of July spectacle for air personnel and installations on the right side of Rapopo.

BOAT SPLIT IN TWO

Some of six enemy medium bombers which attempted to scramble off the airdrome escaped. Most of them did not.

With breathtaking suddenness we were off the target—and away from uncomfortably fierce Jap antiaircraft fire which punctuated the skies around us.

But the attack wasn't over. Henebry didn't stop. With Ellis on the right and Lt. Richard Davis, of Meedford, Ore., on the left, we swooped low over the water, strafing a Jap patrol boat and a large coastal lugger. The patrol boat was split in two, while the lugger was afire and sinking.

Finally, on November 1, 1943, the long-anticipated orders came down from the First Air Task Force near Dobodura. Everyone in the Southwest Pacific Theater expected them. This next mission was to be a maximum effort by all Fifth Air Force attack planes able to carry enough fuel to hit distant Simpson Harbor. We were at last targeting that tempting enemy shipping. Eleven squadrons. The orders included three squadrons of our B-25s, of course.

Because our Third Attack Group was the outfit most experienced in this type of low level, strafing operation, General Freddy Smith of the First Air Task Force tapped us to lead the mission. We had improved our skip bombing techniques by combining minimum altitude masthead bombing tactics with delayed fuse high explosive bombs.

I was serving now as Group Operations Officer and helped coordinate the mission, determining targets, number of aircraft, flight patterns. The job of leading the group that would lead the mission fell on me and my dependable "Notre Dame de Victoire" crew. General Smith and I were newly acquainted—so new that when he announced the lineup he didn't even have my name straight. In assigning the command he referred to me as Major "Henebrin," a name of his own coinage that coincidentally approximated that of the then-popular anti-malarial drug, atabrine.

The command ultimately brought my name, properly pronounced, very positively to the attention of General Kenney who followed the success of this mission intently. Rabaul was my proving ground.

The mission to attack Simpson Harbor was set for the following morning. The 84 planes of the Thirty-Eighth and 345th Groups and our Third were to rendezvous at 9 a.m., at Oro Bay near Dobodura, on the north coast of New Guinea, then head out on course to the St. George's Channel. Four squadrons of the 345th Group would blanket the shore batteries with white phosphorous bombs in an attempt to obstruct the Japanese ground gunners' vision of our harbor approach. By 11 a.m., 80 fighters would be covering us, sweeping the harbor.

Subsequent squadron briefings in preparation for the attack covered additional instructions including emergency and escape procedures involving alternate air strips and rescue submarine locations, a new and welcomed safety precaution.

The morning briefing focused on weather: that morning, CAVU—ceiling and visibility unlimited. Good flying weather all the way.

To finalize the details of executing the mission, particularly to plot the route to and through Simpson Bay, I met with the Group Commanders and flight leaders. Having flown the territory so often in our previous air strip attacks, we agreed there was no secret way to approach the harbor, even with phosphorous cover.

Impossible was an undetectable southeast approach because of our range limitations. Our base position dictated that we arrive from the southwest on a heading of about 40 degrees, depending on the wind and the weather. This route we were forced to adopt would forego our most dependable offensive tactic—surprise. The Japanese were now using the newfangled radar and a network of observation look-outs that would warn of our coming. The target was too well protected to sneak up on it.

Truly, the volcanic mountains dictated our routing. These are the same volcanoes that burned half the town of Rabaul in 1994. At the time of our planned attack they were rumbling but quieter, and high. Those surrounding the harbor almost at its edge, South Daughter, The Mother and North Daughter, rise to more than 2,200 feet.

To fly over their tops and get to water level for strafing and bombing in the close-in harbor would be an extremely steep approach. Dive bombers we were not. Of all possible approaches, a routing over the volcanoes made us the most vulnerable to ground- and ship-based anti-aircraft fire.

We thus chose to fly around the volcanoes rather than over them, hitting our targets on a heading that would take us directly out of the harbor after our bomb run, continuing southwest. Setting up the planes in that pattern would put the attackers on a path toward home, minimizing the need for a radical turn in a combat situation or with a damaged aircraft.

So it was we plotted the course around Cape Gazelle and through the Nordup Gap between the towering volcanoes.

We would be flying in a formation of three-plane V in trail. Passing between the two volcanoes, we could pick out our target ships as we descended down the hill approaching the harbor.

Our standard load for the target and the range of flight was to be two 1,000-pound bombs with four to five second delayed fuses. I slipped an additional 500-pound bomb into my "Notre Dame de Victoire" just in case I ran into something tempting. At take-off we also carried the filled 300-gallon droppable fuel tanks.

At last, a full charge against the harbor at Rabaul. How eager we were. The most important shipping target in the Southwest Pacific. We had heard endlessly about Rabaul, before we had arrived in the theater and continuously since. The toughest target. The best-protected harbor. The Japanese stronghold.

The distance from Dobodura to Rabaul, as the crow flies, is 415 miles and would normally take some two hours. Allowing time to rendezvous, however, to gather into formation and to align ourselves into proper position to make our attack, the distance and time increased to some 450 miles and two and a half hours.

Those first two hours consumed the fuel stored in the non-sealing droppable turret tanks, the fire hazards that we gratefully jettisoned before we reached the attack zone.

Our intent on reaching Simpson Harbor in formation was almost interrupted by the sight of two cruising Japanese destroyers passing through St. George's Channel at high speed, their evasive action churning wakes in the quiet waters. But the temptation to make a pass at these two meaty targets was overcome in favor of keeping our flying pattern until we reached our primary targets, the ships of Simpson Harbor. These destroyers spotted our formations and alerted the naval defenses in the harbor as we swept up the channel.

As I led the formations through the last left turn around The Mother, we were lined up on the northern half of Simpson, hugging the trees of the down slope about a half mile from the eastern side of the harbor. Now, with our first unobstructed look at our targets, we lined up our sights on the vessels beyond.

As promised—what a sight. A hunter's dream. The harbor was alive with ships, tenders and boats. Forewarned, they were armed, ready for our bombardment. This battle would play out to be an attack equal to the Battle of the Bismarck Sea in its devastation—41 ships attacked, 24 bombed, 17 strafed.

We then broke formation, attacking through and over the phosphorus smoke in individual strafing runs. In line with mine, all at 90 degrees to my flight path, were three large ships in a row, one right after another. The setup offered what I thought would be three perfect broadside passes. I had three bombs ready. One for each.

The first, a freighter transport, was the smallest. Beyond it was a larger freighter transport that resembled our liberty ships. The third was the Japanese cruiser Haguro, a fearsome man-o'-war, the largest of the three.

I continued the approach down to water level and started firing the eight fifty-caliber machine guns. I opened the bomb bay doors. As I pulled up to clear the ship mast, I released the first bomb. "Notre Dame" scored a hit.

"Notre Dame De Victoire" hit the two freighters in the background and strafed the heavy cruiser. Anti-aircraft fire from the cruiser damaged the plane during the attack on Simpson Harbor at Rabaul. Note the heavy smoke screen along the harbor, which was carried to give some protection to the attacking planes from shore batteries.

As we cleared the mast I immediately started down sharply to get our guns onto the second ship deck, starting another bomb run, releasing another bomb, pulling up to clear the ship mast. I released the second bomb into the ship midsection just above the water line for maximum penetration.

Great! Another hit.

Two strikes, two hits but now I had problems. The Haguro was in too close to the second transport, making it impossible to push the nose of the B-25 down fast enough to get my guns onto the deck and silence the fire. I had bellied up to the target and was fair game. The ship was firing at us, fire we couldn't return. I couldn't even drop my third bomb.

I looked down and saw her gunners training their pom-pom guns to follow our flight path. They did hit us. And hard. But, because either they had underestimated our speed, now about 250 to 260 miles per hour, or their aim wasn't sharp, they only struck the tail assembly.

The hit caused rudder control problems. I strained to push full right rudder but couldn't push hard enough. Probably some of the control cables were damaged. My co-pilot, Don Frye, also jumped on his right rudder, and fast. The double effort did the job. The plane was again under control.

We stayed on the deck at minimum altitude, low, just above the water, passed across the west side of the harbor and made a turn left around Vulcan Volcano, opposite South Daughter. At a couple of hundred feet, we headed southerly

"Here's Howe" completes a successful attack across Simpson Harbor
at Rabaul and heads back to New Guinea.

These were the tactics . . .

DEPLOYMENT OF FORCES: The strategy of the attack on 2 November against shipping in Simpson Harbor and township installations is depicted in the above diagram.

Numeral **0** indicates the two fighter squadrons assigned to the fighter sweep of the harbor 3 minutes before the bombardment began.

Numeral **1** indicates the fighters and bombers assigned to neutralize shore antiaircraft positions by smoke, strafing fire, and bombs. This force also attacked Lakunai airdrome. Four bombardment squadrons were elements participating in the attack, while two fighter squadrons provided close cover.

Numeral **2** indicates the two squadrons assigned to lead the assault against Simpson Harbor shipping. Another fighter squadron provided close cover. As a diversionary move, these squadrons separated to withdraw from the target area.

Numeral **3** indicates attack route of three bomber squadrons. This force attacked Simpson Harbor approximately 4 minutes after the two leading elements had completed their mission. One fighter squadron gave close cover.

Following the escape of the bombers, fighter forces converged over Vunakanau field and St. George's Channel to cover the bombers.

. . . and these the results

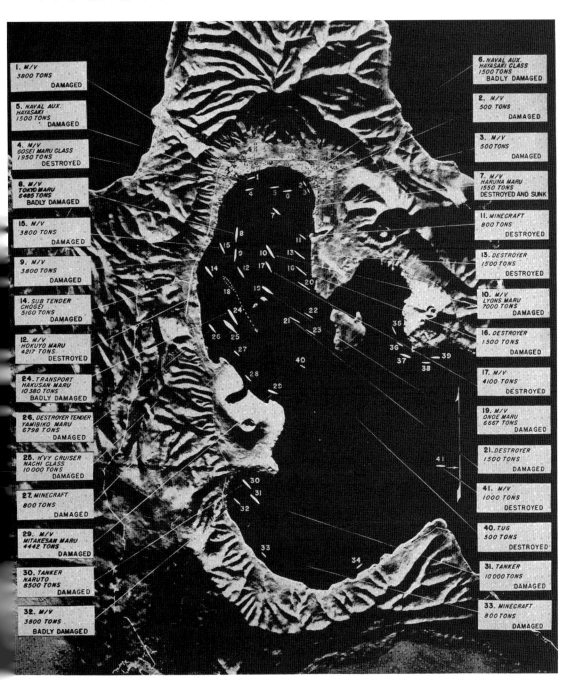

1. M/V
3800 TONS
DAMAGED

5. NAVAL AUX.
HAYASAKI
1500 TONS
DAMAGED

4. M/V
GOSEI MARU CLASS
1950 TONS
DESTROYED

8. M/V
TOKIO MARU
6485 TONS
BADLY DAMAGED

15. M/V
3800 TONS
DAMAGED

9. M/V
3800 TONS
DAMAGED

14. SUB TENDER
CHOGEI
5160 TONS
DAMAGED

12. M/V
HOKUYO MARU
4217 TONS
DESTROYED

24. TRANSPORT
HAKUSAN MARU
10380 TONS
BADLY DAMAGED

26. DESTROYER TENDER
YAMIBIKO MARU
6798 TONS
DAMAGED

25. H'VY CRUISER
NACHI CLASS
10000 TONS
DAMAGED

27. MINECRAFT
800 TONS
DAMAGED

29. M/V
MITAKESAN MARU
4442 TONS
DAMAGED

30. TANKER
NARUTO
8500 TONS
DAMAGED

32. M/V
3800 TONS
BADLY DAMAGED

6. NAVAL AUX.
HAYASAKI CLASS
1500 TONS
BADLY DAMAGED

2. M/V
500 TONS
DAMAGED

3. M/V
500 TONS
DAMAGED

7. M/V
HARUNA MARU
1550 TONS
DESTROYED AND SUNK

11. MINECRAFT
800 TONS
DESTROYED

13. DESTROYER
1500 TONS
DESTROYED

10. M/V
LYONS MARU
7000 TONS
DAMAGED

16. DESTROYER
1500 TONS
DAMAGED

17. M/V
4100 TONS
DESTROYED

19. M/V
ONOE MARU
6667 TONS
DAMAGED

21. DESTROYER
1500 TONS
DAMAGED

41. M/V
1000 TONS
DESTROYED

40. TUG
500 TONS
DESTROYED

31. TANKER
10000 TONS
DAMAGED

33. MINECRAFT
800 TONS
DAMAGED

past the Vunakanau airstrip, our familiar old target. We had one 500-pound bomb left but were too crippled to make a firing pass. Instead we jettisoned the third and last bomb and swung a little right to a heading of about 225 degrees, the reciprocal of our inbound heading from Dobodura. We left a developing sweep of conflagration as planes continued emerging from the Gap, swooping down on to the harbor, attacking their chosen targets with all the firepower they had and exiting southwest.

As we moved toward the Solomon Sea and home, a Japanese fighter plane, one of the 125 to 150 estimated to be in the skies, jumped us. Our rear turret guns had been knocked out by the Haguro. So we had no defensive fire and not much speed because of our damaged rudders and tail section. Our assigned fighter cover was busy at higher altitudes and could offer no relief to our immediate problem. Those pilots probably hadn't even seen us being jumped.

The Japanese fighter made a pass from our rear and hit the left engine hard. He knocked it out quickly. He must have been firing 20 millimeter guns, standard equipment for Japanese Navy fighters. The engine immediately lost power.

I pulled the power back and shut off the fuel to the damaged engine. The oil pressure gauge went to zero as I reached for the red "feather" button but the prop on the shot-up engine wouldn't respond because we had lost oil pressure so fast. Worse, the windmilling propeller was causing considerable drag.

We went to full power on our good right engine. Frye and I, attempting to maximize the power, pushed the throttle and the rpm controls so far forward we almost bent them.

The Japanese fighter left before he finished us off. Why, I don't know. Maybe he didn't want to stray any further from his home base. Maybe he thought he had shot us down. Maybe we were lucky.

But he hadn't. I checked with the rest of the crew to find everyone okay. All that enemy activity and everyone okay! I was grateful, astonished, happy and relieved.

With the crew whole, the major concern became maintaining airspeed, a near impossibility with all the damage we had sustained, our problems topped off by a windmilling prop. But the good engine at full throttle was running like a 21-jewel watch, keeping us airborne.

The B-25 is an obstinate warplane but we were dying. Our speed was down to 125 mph at a couple hundred feet with quite a distance to fly to the nearest. alternate airstrip in friendly territory. To lighten up, we began throwing overboard everything we didn't need. We jettisoned several hundred rounds of ammunition, the rear power turret gun barrels, tools, flashlights—anything that wasn't tied down.

We determined from our charts that the nearest land was Kiriwina Island, some 300 miles south southwest of Rabaul, a low-lying coral island in the Trobriand group in the Solomon Sea housing an RAAF wing. It boasted a couple of airstrips of sorts, completed mid-October. We were flying a few degrees to the right so we adjusted our heading to 210 degrees. I estimated our position to

Lee Van Atta and Dick Ellis after the November 2 raid on Simpson Harbor at Rabaul. The story on the following page was filed by Van Atta, who rode along in "Seabiscuit" during the attack.

U. S. Raid on Rabaul Demoralizing to Japs

American Airmen Pitted Finest Offensive Weapon Against Nips to Win Important Victory

By LEE VAN ATTA

ABOARD AN AMERICAN MITCHELL BOMBER EN ROUTE FROM RABAUL, Nov. 2 (Delayed) (INS)—Less than an hour ago American airmen pitted their finest offensive weapon against Nippon's most formidable defensive weapons. The Americans won the round in the most brutal aerial battering ever dealt Japanese shipping.

For 25 minutes the United States Mitchell bombers fought Japanese Zeros, flak ships and land and sea anti-aircraft batteries to win their way to the assigned target. For another 30 minutes they waged unceasing combat with what seemed unending streams of Zero and Messerschmitt fighters to reach home base.

The craft of this correspondent returned looking like a sieve.

The American craft attacked and destroyed almost all their objectives in the most demanding mission ever assigned to youthful United States bombardment and fighter pilots. In the grueling man-made hell they destroyed or damaged over 94,000 tons of enemy shipping in Simpson Harbor.

It is almost impossible to analyze every thought and impression which flowed through the mind of any single man who witnessed the assault in those harrowing minutes which seemed like eternity.

But the general impression is that Pearl Harbor on Dec. 7, 1941, could never have looked like Simpson anchorage today. Everywhere ships lay mortally wounded as the American raiders soared from their objectives. Everywhere there were pyramids of flame and crumbling, searing hunks of steel.

Capt. Richard Ellis, of Laurel, Del., veteran of 65 strafing missions against the foe and youngest command pilot in the southwest Pacific war theater, accounted for two vessels destroyed before the eyes of this correspondent. The ships were knocked out by a technique of attack few men ever have witnessed.

WHOLE SKY ABLAZE

Bombs exploded and mingled with anti-aircraft bursts until it seemed that the whole sky was ablaze. At least four large Jap cruisers maneuvered in the bay and fired tremendous salvoes at Capt. Ellis' craft.

The anti-aircraft fire was so thick that Ellis said he practically flew through it on his instruments.

Aboard his Mitchell was Maj. John (Jock) Henebry of Plainfield, Ill., courageous command pilot, who has been associated with every outstanding attack in this theater from the Bismarck Sea through Wewak and Rabaul.

One of the most trying moments came when his Mitchell ahead of Ellis' craft was seen to lose altitude fast. It began dropping everything that could be put overboard after the apparent failure of its left engine. Ellis' ship had to swerve to avoid the falling objects from inside the plane.

The approach called for the planes to go down the New Britain-New Ireland Channel and swing over the towering Rabaul volcanoes and thence to drop in over the harbor at a 90-degree angle.

The first combat came just off New Ireland where geysers from the sea told the fliers that the escorting Lightning fighter craft, led by Capt. Gerald Johnson of Eugene, Ore., had sighted trouble and were gunning for the same.

ACK-ACK PLENTIFUL

The aerial fighting began above just a second later. Then came ack-ack in plentiful quantities from the shore batteries of New Ireland which burst among the formation. Less than half a mile away a destroyer surprised in mid-channel opened fire with everything it had.

The American planes gathered in battle formation. The advance elements of Mitchells prepared to pound the positions at Lakunai airstrip and along the harbor shore.

The planes swept in between the mother and daughter volcanoes which hypothetically should have protected Simpson Harbor from low-level attack. Immediately those rugged, magnificant-looking towers af active craters burst into life—not volcanic, but anti-aircraft life.

Capt. Ellis, considered along with Henebry one of the calmest but deadliest pilots, opened fire as his craft began to climb out over the steep slopes. Then suddenly the whole panorama of ship-teeming Simpson Harbor could be seen ahead. The prospect of what awaited these ships was itself terrifying.

Cruisers and destroyers were maneuvering in the harbor and belching flak salvoes. The Mitchell lead elements swept through the ack-ack defenses to pummel Lakunai and the township itself with bombs and strafing fire in an effort to thoroughly confuse the foe.

DID WILD JUMPS

The air speed indicators of the Mitchells did wild jumps as the craft tore downward over the volcano ridges and the ships came into clear focus. At an altitude substantially below 50 feet Ellis' plane made its first run on a 5,000-ton cargo vessel and for a time one would think that the Mitchell would be unable to stagger up over the ship's masts. The forward guns raked the wheelhouse with a blistering barrage. A blinking light indicated that the first 1,000-pound bomb was away.

Ellis yanked back the controls as a Lightning pilot might and jammed them forward again. The ship was back just over the water once more and beginning a second run—this time on the biggest merchantman in the harbor, a two-stacked 10,000-tonner.

The plane knifed across the bow of the heavy cruiser, which was belching salvoes from its naval and ack-ack guns. How the fire missed no one will ever know. The plane swept onto the target—invitingly luminous with smoking flak fire—inches above the water. Again the forward guns chattered and again tracers did flaming loops into the wheelhouse and deck positions.

1,000-POUNDER LOOSENED

Ellis and Co-pilot Lt. John Dean grabbed the controls simultaneously and then, with a stomach-thudding heave, pulled the plane up over the vessel and loosed the second 1,000-pounder. The rear gunner confirmed that the bomb landed square amidships. When last seen the vessel was slashed in half and sinking like a 10-ton rock in Crater Lake.

Then the plane staggered "up hill" over the ridge surrounding Simpson Harbor on the south and again Ellis' forward guns chattered against the hillock position. Within seconds the plane was in a rain squall, and then it emerged to face a force of Jap Zeros greater than Ellis had seen before.

Eight Zeros tacked onto the tail. Enemy fire looked into the navigator's window near where this correspondent sat and riddled his reading material entitled incidentally, "Fifty Famous Thrillers." More shellfire ripped into the engines, the tail wings and fuselage.

Masterly, cool firing by Staff Sgt. Emmor Mullenhaur of Lima, Ohio, and James Bowling of Hamilton, Ohio, who accounted for at least one Zero, plus Ellis' cool and consistently sound and evasive maneuvering gave the crew those vital seconds so necessary to permit the craft to rejoin the original attacking elements which had swung miles ahead.

The craft was able to rejoin the elements because Mullenhaur outguessed on every turn the foe's potential firepower and because Ellis outguessed on every turn the enemy's tactical capabilities.

As the plane escaped off the New Britain coast those aboard could see bitter dogfights perhaps 3,000 feet above between Lightnings and Zeros. It was almost an hour away from the targets before the Zeros finally departed and Ellis' plane was free to continue its way unmolested. The crew knew then that they would be home before long despite the fact there was a 20-millimeter shell hole through the right engine.

be 70 to 80 miles from the initial target leaving more than 200 miles of flying to dry land.

The good right engine continued to purr. Although shot up and in obvious trouble, we were holding our course. Frye and I still held the right rudder pedal hard, keeping the plane under control. We were able to maintain our 125 mph with a very slight nose down attitude. Obviously this could not last forever or we would be under water.

Curious thoughts crept through my mind. I had been flying around the Pacific islands now for a year and a half but had never flown a seaplane nor landed on the water. It looked easy. The water would be warm. Were there sharks in the Solomon Sea? Knowing the configuration of the B-25, I thought it should make a good water landing. The wings joined the fuselage at its midpoint. The underslung belly would serve as a pontoon.

I would leave the landing gear up. A smooth belly would skim the water surface. Why would I need wheels to land on water anyway? I'm now flying a seaplane. It wasn't intended to be a seaplane but that's what our B-25 was destined to become.

We'd dropped our bomb load and will have used our fuel. We're light. But how long would our lightened plane stay afloat? It shouldn't take us very long to abandon it.

We all have life vests and a six-man inflatable rubber life raft that would pop out of its compartment if we don't damage the release mechanism during the landing.

The closer we are to Kiriwina when we ditch, the better our chances of being picked up.

A surprise interrupted my speculations. On our left at our same altitude was another B-25, a reassuring sight. He may not be able to keep us flying but if we go down at sea, he could report our position, making our rescue an easier task.

The B-25 pulled closer and I could read "Here's Howe" lettered around the scantily clad gal holding a glass of champagne in a toast to my pal Chuck Howe. Chuck and I had flown a lot of combat together. He was sticking close. He had seen how shot up our rear was and knew more keenly than we did what bad shape we were in.

The "Notre Dame de Victoire" was my third or fourth assigned plane since arriving in New Guinea. It came to me with a name and accompanying nose art of a lurid nature. Father John Wood, a Viatorian priest assigned as chaplain to the Group, strongly suggested that since I was a Notre Dame graduate I rename the plane "Our Lady of Victory."

"Fine with me," I agreed and he arranged to have a nose artist repaint the new name on the plane. Then further he advised me that the chief of chaplains for the Fifth Air Force, Father Gerhardt, was due to visit our Dobodura base and he brought him over to christen the plane with its venerable name. A very

Father John Wood, Group Chaplain, and John Henebry standing in front of "Notre Dame De Victoire"

blessed beginning for a plane that a few weeks later was flying a doomed journey to Kiriwina Island, tracked in its final moments by a shameless party girl acting as its angel.

Our airspeed was decreasing and we were losing what little altitude we had. We were right about 100 mph and our altitude had passed under 100 feet. But what we were doing was about all we could do in our world of seemingly

Sergeant Garber, Sergeant Mullovich, Lieutenant Murphy, John Henebry and
Father Gerhardt, Fifth Air Force Chaplain, at the christening of "Notre Dame De Victoire"

unending sky and water. We had been in this deteriorating condition for more than an hour and were straining to see land.

Our charts had indicated no mountains on Kiriwina—a coral atoll—pretty flat—no volcanoes. That is bad and good. Bad because we wouldn't be able to see it until we were in close. Good because we wouldn't need to gain altitude to approach the airstrip.

We had descended to just about zero altitude, right above the water over a reasonably calm sea. So low, Howe would later describe the long, narrow wake we were making in the water. Our airspeed was holding fairly well at around 100. I realized we were being kept airborne by an air cushion created when the downward pressure of our plane, particularly its wings moving through the air, reacted off the water surface. A very helpful phenomenon, indeed.

Although the situation was tenuous, we were making progress toward Kiriwina when the inevitable occurred—fire started in the left engine. Because the fuel to that damaged engine had been shut off, there were no flames, only sparks and a trail of smoke. I had been waiting for it. We continuously had attempted to feather the dead engine to stop it from windmilling. Windmilling causes drag. Windmilling also generates a friction heat that ultimately starts fires when a "dry" engine is allowed to continue spinning long enough. We had never been able to feather that engine and it had been windmilling since outside Rabaul.

But straight ahead, our navigation being correct, on the horizon we saw what at first looked like a shadow. We were in a drastic situation, we needed to be ashore and were greatly relieved to see that friendly land.

What we saw was an almost flat coral atoll rimmed with palm trees obscuring our sighting of the airstrip. I have seen impressively high palm trees but in our circumstances these were giants. They presented a problem I hadn't anticipated. Can I gain enough altitude to clear them, probably 150 feet required at this slow speed, and still keep control of the airplane? What. happens if I pull up? Will I lose the lifting effect of the air cushion we were flying on? What if, when I do pull up, if I can, and clear the palm trees, if I can, I am not lined up with the strip to continue my approach? In that case would I be able to turn and still keep control? Each of these "what ifs" involved extreme risk.

The next option, the Kiriwina beach, was invitingly on our left, but too narrow for landing.

I made a quick decision. Ditch in the surf. How? Upwind across the waves or along the top of the swell? The weather was good. The surf was moderate. We were running almost parallel to the beach and could land in a trough between breakers. But even in the best of circumstances, ditching is hazardous. Crew injuries can result when unsecured equipment has not been jettisoned. Ditched planes stay afloat an unpredictable amount of time, hopefully long enough here to give my crew time to enter a lifeboat. In spite of the dangers, ditching was my decision.

Because of the rudder control problem, Frye and I were still holding both feet on the right rudder controls to keep the plane from turning sharply left. When I pulled back the power on our operative right engine in preparation to land, the plane started to turn sharply. As one, Frye and I quickly eased off the right rudder control and reduced power on the right engine just enough to hold our path straight for landing. The B-25, known to be easy to handle, lived up to its reputation and made a beautiful wheels-up belly landing.

End of flight, but not end of our challenge. We had to get out of the sinking plane. That turned out to be easy. I pulled the six-man life raft release and opened the overhead pilot escape hatch. The hatch popped right off and Frye and I dove forward through the opening.

From under the water, trying to reach the surface, I bumped my head on a mass above me. My first thought was that the plane had cracked up on landing and I was caught in the wreckage. Feeling around, I determined that I was under the wing between the nacelle and the fuselage. I repeated over and over again, "Be calm; be calm," pulling down on the two lower strings to inflate my Mae West life vest. I quickly surfaced behind the trailing edge of the wing. I was in good shape and looked for the six-man raft.

I could not find it. The release had not activated. It had not come out of its compartment near the top of the left side of the fuselage above the wing. But "Notre Dame de Victoire" was still floating. I climbed up on the wing. I reached the hatch handle. It was stuck and I couldn't open the cover. The closest implement at hand was my .45 pistol, secure in my shoulder holster. Holding it by its barrel, I used it as a hammer, banging the flat hatch handle to release the raft.

It worked well and fast. The hatch opened, the raft popped out and automatically inflated, knocking me back into the water. For the second time, grabbing onto the raft I pulled myself up and climbed in. The first one aboard.

Bobbing all around me, all safe in their life vests, were the rest of our six-man crew. Frye and four others—a navigator, a luxury allowed because we were leading such a major mission, a top turret gunner and two photographers—answered to the "roll call" as "Present and accounted for." They all started paddling and swimming and soon all six of us were safely in the raft.

The plane was still floating, but sinking. Within ten minutes, the nose disappeared below the water leaving the tail gracefully extended into the air. Soon that too slid under the surface. We sat, sad and secure on the bobbing raft watching it. After four hours and 20 minutes of anxiety, we were relieved to be intact.

No one would record the sinking. "God dammit," cursed one of the photographers, "there go all the pictures I took, film, cameras and all." And before us was the final dramatic undocumented disappearing image of a plane engineered to respond to every move we had been trained to take in an emergency, bringing us to safety, taking the camera down with it.

But in the overall assessment, these were minor concerns. We were all grateful to be afloat. Of the six guys downed, a small scratch on my forehead was the only blood. The only pain was a crewman's dislocated shoulder. One scratch, one ache, one airplane. That was all. A bunch of lucky guys.

And then satisfaction set in. A feeling inexpressible then and now. We had flown more than 400 miles leading a major mission to hit the toughest target in the Pacific involving tons of enemy shipping, personally sunk or seriously damaged two enemy ships, got shot up by a cruiser, got jumped by a Japanese fighter plane, lost an engine which eventually caught fire, flew a crippled B-25 300 miles over water toward a blip of an island with a reputation, unknown to us then, of being probably the most vulgar and sexually oriented in the Solomon Sea, landed in the water just short of the island airstrip with minor injury. Happy aviators, we were.

Floating some two to three hundred yards from the beach in a fairly calm sea early in the afternoon, we were not yet putting our minds to our next move when we spotted a speed boat coming at us full bore. We watched it approach and quickly identified it as a U.S. Navy PT boat. Millions of square miles of sea and a PT boat pulls up along side our raft.

The skipper hailed us and as we clambered aboard he checked that the six of us were OK. We crowded around him and his crew, shaking hands in gratitude.

We asked what brought them to us so fast and the skipper explained that well before we landed, he had spotted the trailing smoke from our plane.

"I'll take you over to a jetty two or three miles up the Kiriwina coast; you are in friendly territory," he assured us. He astonished us with an offer of Torpedo Juice. No one questioned the safety of the ingredients. No one questioned Navy regulations. Torpedo Juice, made from the alcohol used as fuel in torpedoes mixed with a little water, is damn good in such unconventional surroundings. Well, maybe not damn good but drinkable and we welcomed the chance to toast our rescuers.

The moments and the coastline rushed by. The young, heroic, good looking skipper and his accommodating crew headed toward the jetty where the finale of our adventure was unfolding.

As we approached, we saw Yanks standing on it and as we drew close I could see that it was Captain Howe who had stuck with us through our water landing and proceeded to the airstrip we had been heading for. From the airstrip, he had borrowed a Jeep and drove to the jetty to meet us.

Another round of handshakes, thanks and farewells for the skipper and his PT crew as we climbed onto the jetty, piled into the Jeep, drove to the airstrip, boarded "Here's Howe" and headed for Dobodura, our home base about 175 miles away.

We were an hour-and-a-half late getting back to base, but still in time for debriefing. Seven other B-25s were down, taking with them 26 enemy fighters and ten flying boats. Nine fighters lost. Forty-five pilots and crew killed or missing.

Sitting at the bottom of the sea after 12 minutes of destruction: 114 thousand tons of enemy sea power—one Japanese heavy cruiser, one destroyer tender, one submarine tender, three destroyers, two naval auxiliary craft, three mine sweepers, 16 merchant vessels, two tankers, a barge and a tug. Sixty-eight enemy planes were destroyed in the air or on the field. Another 300,000 tons of shipping were damaged. Thus ended a triumphant day. Later General Kenney would grant that this, "the most successful week of the war in the Southwest Pacific . . . belonged to the airmen." Rabaul ended Japanese aspirations over conquest of the Pacific.

Soon after, General Kenney and Father Gerhardt were reviewing Fifth Air Force news and Gerhardt commented that he had blessed Henebry's new plane. Kenney retorted, "Good enough, but the plane was shot down." Kenney threatened to keep him and his holy water away from my next airplane. Gerhardt responded, "Nobody was hurt. That sounds like a blessing to me."

15

Whiskey Drop

MID-NOVEMBER 1943. A regiment of the First Marine Division that helped recapture and secure Guadalcanal was preparing for its next operation. Its Oro Bay staging camp to retrain and reequip its men was near our Third Attack Group's Dobodura base.

We also were reorganizing and retraining after a strenuous few months hitting Japanese shipping off Cape Gloucester and Rabaul Harbor and trying to neutralize enemy airfields. Our concentration was on new northwestward targets. Japanese were on the run; we were right on their tails.

During the respite, our life style took on some signs of civility. Females were now part of the scene: the Army had established a hospital nearby, bringing in its nurses. Our jungle neighborhood became livelier and certainly lovelier. However, the jungle remained just that. Tents and straw-roofed huts were not much of an environment for gracious socializing.

The mood was exuberant. A new, fresh lineup was developing to jack up the few of us who began in Brisbane. Most of the Third who had originally fought so hard with so little had perished in battle or mishap, been transferred out of the theater or had rotated home. A few original noncoms also remained, continuing on in their administrative or service responsibilities. The atmosphere was now bright with the confidence of victory.

At last, after two years of battle in this sweltering, water-logged portion of the globe, the world we came from finally was focusing some attention on our contributions to the struggle, sending us entertainment. Gary Cooper was the first to find our island, leading a USO troop including Una Merkle, Phyllis Brooks and a guitar player, unknown then and unknown now. The low-keyed show thrilled the troops. Cooper became our song and dance man putting his sophisticated twist on "Rum and Coca Cola" and "Lay That Pistol Down, Babe." The urbane man, the glitzy troop, the fanciful songs—it was all so out of place in this primitive landscape. The tunes were so new to us who were more in touch with ship movements than show biz.

During this peaceful interlude, orders came from the First Air Task Force, our operational advanced headquarters, to get acquainted with the Marines who were camped down the coast at Oro Bay and I brought our Third Attack Group operational people over to do just that.

The Marine liaison officer serving as their "meet and greet" officer was Captain Frank Farrell, a former New York World newsman and, following the war, a columnist for that paper. In that get-acquainted process we learned that our Third would be providing close air-ground support for an upcoming amphibious Marine landing on New Britain, across the Solomon Sea, and would continue to support their offensive push inland.

The initial landing on Arawe off the south coast would be the first Allied land invasion in that territory. New Britain continued to be a vital holding in the Japanese plan to isolate Australia. The enemy had fortified the island heavily and had sustained continuous attack against Rabaul on the east supporting activity in the Solomons and Cape Gloucester on the west end supporting its flagging New Guinea offense.

But a concerned Captain Farrell exposed his superior officers' lack of interest in and cooperation with the air support being planned for the invasion. I found that attitude strange. Were I an infantryman making an amphibious invasion of heavily fortified enemy territory, I would want all the help my military could offer.

The reluctance of Farrell's commander was based in distrust of our ability to bomb and strafe accurately when closely covering invading troops. The concern was legitimate. Often in invasions poor planning and bad judgments made in the heat of battle had caused tragic accidents.

Our Third Attack Group was different. Conducting such support operations was one of the specialties of our attack squadrons. We were outstanding in such operations and were confident of our ability.

The invading Marines did not share our optimism and, even though our assignment came from higher headquarters, we needed to convince these Marines that we of the Third could provide effective support during their landing and subsequent incursion into this significant enemy objective.

Farrell suggested we meet with the executive officer of his Marine outfit, Lieutenant Colonel Paul "Chesty" Puller, and advised we have our presentation well-prepared because Puller was "one tough cookie who would be asking a lot of questions."

Farrell filled me in on Puller—what an amazing fighter he was. A career Marine, he had entered the Corps after World War I and had been chasing the Japanese around the Pacific since Pearl Harbor. Guadalcanal had been his latest campaign. He was short, stocky, pug-nosed and ram-rod straight. The name "Chesty" was a natural.

I was ready, eager to impress Puller. I set up a flight demonstration that could show him what we do. The fire power exercise used our B-25s and A-20s dramatically pummelling a nearby range. I put Colonel Puller in the co-pilot's seat of my B-25 to let him feel the power of eight fifty-caliber machine guns firing and a couple of bombs hitting a practice target. This was language he understood and appreciated.

Following all that roar and thunder Puller and Farrell met with us at our Dobodura group headquarters where we explained the preliminary procedures we employ for such a cover operation as their New Britain invasion.

The areas both at the beach and inland would be photographed completely and carefully from the air. From the photographs we would create an indexed grid map—numbers representing half mile increments across the top and letters down the side. Ground Marines and our pilots would carry these identical maps.

Before battle, radio communication would be established between the troops on the ground and our pilots in flight, circling and holding within radio range in an area nearby.

When Marines on the ground ran into opposition or an identifiable enemy strong point, they could talk directly to the holding pilot and pinpoint the problem. The conversation would be as simple as "ground to Blue Flight—six delta— high west." To both that meant trouble in the northwest corner of the half mile square indicated by 6-D. Since the area once inland from the beach was mostly coconut palms or rain forest, the maps established position positively. The Japanese had to be among the palms or within the rain forest. Rarely would you catch this enemy in the few openings the terrain provided.

It became obvious that we knew our stuff. We convinced these Marines and their leader quickly. Their attitudes toward the crazy fly-boys changed.

After that personal demonstration flight we returned to our group headquarters for a debriefing. During an intense question and answer session a lot of the concerns about such an operation were eliminated. A tough old bird who knew his business, Puller recognized our ability to provide a layer of protection over his troops. He grew more and more appreciative as the talking continued.

The display and discussions done, I prevailed upon Doc Gilmore, now our flight surgeon, to break loose with some medicinal combat whiskey rations to formalize the harmony we had reached. Doc and I shared a shack at Dobodura and he provided this gracious conclusion to a successful day. Since whiskey "doth loosen the tongue," Doc Gilmore's contribution closed up the great distance we had gone to understand fully each other's concerns.

Medicinal spirits were a recent innovation in our war, replacing homemade jungle juice. After two years of combat, the policy of supplying such had just been introduced and was a welcomed gesture even though the allocations were tightly secured in heavily guarded tents.

A busy month of December followed. Our Third completed a number of preliminary search and destroy missions on New Britain and the north coast of New Guinea, concentrating on Cape Gloucester and Finschhafen. Since the Marines were scheduling a landing around Christmas at Arawe, preparations grew intense.

During my involvement with the Marine landing, I discovered that a Notre Dame classmate, Dick Kelly, was a captain and tank commander preparing to go ashore with these men. He introduced me to tank driving in a one and only experience that quickly convinced me that I would rather be driving an airplane.

Kelly victoriously completed the New Britain invasion. He then moved on with the Marines to Palau Island where a Japanese sniper surprised him on a dirt road as he commanded his tank company from an exposed position, his head and shoulders protruding from the hatch of the lead tank. Before he even reached the battle, he had been shot and killed.

By mid-December we had learned the extent of the entire ground force operation against New Britain at its western end near Cape Gloucester. The Eighth Army would be staging a major amphibious attack on the north coast. Our Marines, smaller in number than the Eighth Army's troops, were to land on the south coast at Arawe in a diversionary action.

The First Air Task Force suggested that we, as the Marine's supporting air power, do a low level flight reconnaissance of the area to become familiar with the neighborhood.

At this point in the war new A-20s direct from the Douglas factory were replacing our old well-worn A-20s and B-25s from the first days of combat. The Third would now be all A-20s as it had been before the war. A great airplane to fly, the A-20 was lighter than the B-25 with the same two Wright R-2600, 1700 horsepower engines. It carried a single pilot and a rear gunner. These new models were smaller, faster and more maneuverable than our faithful old B-25s.

Doc Gilmore thought it his duty to fly on combat missions now and then to experience the conditions that confronted the flight crews and better understand their problems. Doc relished these adventures and he asked to go along on this reconnaissance flight.

A passenger in the A-20 can stand in the bomb bay directly behind the pilot with his head and shoulders positioned under the cockpit canopy. In this ringside seat, the passenger sees everything the pilot sees.

Doc stood there when we set up the flight of three A-20s and flew out of Dobodura about 150 miles across the sea to the south coast of New Britain, east of Gloucester. Because of the perfect weather, even at low altitudes we could see for miles. Then we cruised westerly past Arawe, past the double-peaked Mount Tangi and, appreciating our proximity to the enemy, found ourselves approaching the enemy's Cape Gloucester airstrip.

We knew this neighborhood. It was very near where we had sunk two destroyers and had shot down a Japanese transport plane in September.

This day was very quiet. No activity. We had heard that the Japanese were trying to evacuate the area. With that in mind and with Doc at my shoulder, I decided to make a low pass over the Gloucester airfield and was astonished by the sight of an elegant Zeke fighter sitting near a clump of trees not far from the airstrip. A perfect plane being carefully worked on by a couple of Japanese mechanics. Tempting me.

I see that plane still as though it came into my view this morning. A bright green splash of metal trimmed smartly in black and imperiously displaying the garish rising sun emblem. Its grandeur indicated it was the proud property of some military hot shot—perhaps a Group Commander.

I ruined that hot shot's day by disfiguring that beautiful paint job. One burst from my A-20's six fifty-caliber machine guns instantly spilled fuel on fire over the ground. How fast it burned. I had time for a couple repeat bursts from my guns on that one pass and blew that beauty to pieces.

Maybe the plane didn't have self-sealing tanks or maybe it had ferry tanks on board. Something fed an explosion that provided a good show for my passenger. I was enjoying it too.

Then the engines quit. We were right on the deck reaching the end of the airstrip with the blazing plane below and behind us when the A-20 engines quit. Unlike the B-25, the A-20s' supplemental gas supply is controlled by a manual switch at the pilot's fingertips. Mine found it fast. The engines started up again immediately and we jubilantly returned to Dobodura to make our reconnaissance report and to prepare for the Marine Arawe operation.

We learned the Marines would hit the beach Christmas eve and would be embarking at Oro Bay in a few days. Our group had prepared fully. Nothing remained but to wish them well.

We drove over to the Marine camp to see Puller and Farrell. They pointed out that we fly-boys, come Christmas, would be back at Dobodura enjoying a heated feast of a meal while they would be at their new jungle address in a rain forest chasing Japanese—or vice versa.

I reminded them that during the Christmas combat our mission took us airborne to be at their service. With our grid maps I suggested we could be even more accommodating to them than imagined. Puller said, "Yeah, how?"

If the landing goes well, I promised, I would drop a bottle of Australian whiskey for their Christmas celebration. Puller's skeptical response was, "How the hell are you going to do that?"

I explained that once we had pinpointed their headquarters we could parachute the bottle down their chimney.

"Sure," Puller doubtfully growled, "we'll look forward to that!"

I did obtain a rarity, a fifth of Australian whiskey. Old Corio is not a distinguished label, a mere step above no whiskey at all. But under the circumstances it would be relished. I also easily found an empty fifty-caliber ammunition box, wrapped the old Corio in sponge rubber, sealed it in the heavy wood box and fastened a small parachute from a parafrag bomb to ease the fall.

Everything was working well. A couple of days after Puller and company landed, we were able to locate his regimental command post on our grid maps and we planned the drop.

I piloted the A-20 with the Christmas cargo in the care of rear gunner Sergeant Caesar Bocchino. His instructions were to stay on the intercom and when he received word from me he was—pronto—to drop the box.

I located the proper grid. I gave him the word. He let the whiskey go through the lower door just below the power gun turret. He reported the parachute opening and the drop looking good.

From below on the ridges of Cape Gloucester it looked good, too. A marine officer found the delivery wrapped in its sponge rubber, packed in its strong wooden box attached to its parachute from a parafrag bomb marked SAFE HAND and addressed to Marine Captain Farrell. It was a fine display of minimum altitude bombing on a pin-pointed position.

Some two weeks later we received a weather-beaten note from Captain Farrell thanking us for the Christmas present and describing the scene in the coconut grove with the officers and staff passing around the Old Corio, enthusiastically toasting their Air Corps protectors and suppliers. We had doubly proven our worth.

About 40 years after the great Christmas drop, I was playing golf at Green Tree in Florida near Orlando. I had just paid my greens fee and was waiting on the first tee when the starter approached asking, "Are you Henebry from New Guinea?"

"Yes, I am," I responded.

"Were you in the Third Attack Group?"

"Yes, I was," I responded.

"I'm the A-20 gunner who dropped the whiskey to the Marines, Sergeant Bocchino." He was the now retired Bucky Bocchino from New Jersey, working during the winter as the Green Tree starter.

Field Promotion

I was at Dobodura when the call came over the land line to fly back over the Owen Stanley Range for a Commanders Conference at Port Moresby's Fifth Bomber Command Headquarters.

The day-long session ended with our trekking up the hill out of the heat to Colonel "Jungle Jim" Davies quarters for beer and booze. Davies had brought together his Group Commanders—me, the most recently appointed of the five, Ken Rogers, Harry Hawthorn, Clint True and Larry Tanburg. Davies, his staff and Pappy Gunn, up from Brisbane, had spent an intense day with us discussing war philosophy and plans and we were ready to relax.

With hardly enough time to shed our shoes, we spotted Major General Ennis Whitehead, commander of this Fifth Air Force advance headquarters, moving up the hill followed by MacArthur's head airman, Lieutenant General George C. Kenney, with their small entourage. Some party.

The conversation of the evening was soon halted with Kenney's question to Davies, "Has Jock received his promotion to lieutenant colonel yet?" I was a fairly new major and eagerly listened for the response. "Not yet," Davis replied, "but it's all right with me."

"We should do something about that," Kenney announced, asking if anyone had an extra silver leaf, the insignia for that rank.

Pappy Gunn, the colorful creator of our low altitude B-25s, unfastened the leaf on his shirt and offered it to Kenney who pinned it on me, now standing in overwhelmed silence, with a simple "Congratulations."

He turned to his secretary and said, "Cut those orders for Jock in the morning." Kenney kept close track of his "boys" and my extensive combat flying had put me on his list.

We all went back to our booze and beer.

General Kenney pins the silver leaf on John Henebry
with his promotion to Lieutenant Colonel at Port Moresby.

This was the airman's way, without the drama of trench warfare to serve as backdrop. Short of being actually airborne during the "ceremony," having the theater air commander do the honors in a jungle base was drama enough for me.

The next morning I flew the Owen Stanley Range again, a brand new 25-year old Group Commander and now a lieutenant colonel. This war was being good to me, a war that was being won by guys just like me—guys who liked to fly planes and shoot guns.

Just a few weeks earlier, in November of 1943, 1 had become the Commander of the Third Attack Group and its Eighth, Thirteenth, Eighty-Ninth and Ninetieth Squadrons. Their histories strung back into World War I and the French campaign when they were consolidated into the Third. Through the Air Corps developmental years between wars the Third had such Air Corps legends as General Kenney, Jimmy Doolittle, Carl "Tooey" Spaatz, Jim Davies, Ennis Whitehead, Bob Strickland and recently D. P. Hall, who had rotated home after leading several of the inaugural low level B-25 strafing missions.

Outside the "Tropical Paradise" at Dobodura are, left to right: Colonel D. P. Hall, Brigadier General Ramey, Colonel Davies, Major Good, Lieutenant Colonel Downs, Major Wilkens, and Major Henebry

And now me, fresh out of a major mission, facing the most responsibility I had known in my couple dozen years of life. Looking back now from my 80+ year perch, 25 seems quite young to command the 5,000 men and 64 planes of the Third, but at 25, I viewed moving up the command ladder so swiftly totally in keeping with the pace of war. A captain one and a half years out of flight school. A major eight months later. Now a lieutenant colonel, not yet three years after a graduation when all I wanted was an airplane to fly.

My first squadron commander was a man in his forties, a man who had been collecting flying experience in the military as many years as I had been alive. I had been named a squadron commander at 25 with only two years of military flying on my log.

All four squadron commanders in my Group were about my age. My year and a half of flying combat out of New Guinea bases with the Third Attack Group was as long a time flying as any other pilot in the Third. The only exception had been the flying record of Major Ray Wilkins, commanding officer of the Eighth Squadron who earlier that month had been shot down in the air war over Rabaul, fatally crashing into the harbor. It had brought Wilkins the Congressional Medal of Honor, awarded posthumously.

Death or rotation kept the average a young age. In the early stages of the war, after 50 missions a pilot or crewman was eligible to go home, ending his tour of duty, while the military was expanding and jobs kept opening up. I never considered rotating home as long as this war raged. I spent much of my conversation trying to convince others to stay in the fight but many of the

Major Raymond H. Wilkens' Congressional Medal of Honor was awarded posthumously

combatants had had enough of the jungle and the jeopardy. They never wanted to be away from home. They didn't want to be on an island in the Pacific. They didn't want to be flying combat. They took the first opportunity to rotate, usually by completing missions or by injury. Pilots went home. New pilots replaced them. Very seldom did a pilot eligible for rotation return to combat.

Chuck Howe was one of the few. Chuck was a fireman from Santa Barbara. His hometown newspapers followed his spectacular career in the Pacific. He bravely completed his 50 missions and was slated to go home with well-deserved hero status. But Chuck was one of our Group's best combat pilots so Doc and I took him down to Dobodura's idyllic inlet where we would swim in the ocean safely protected against the sharks by strung netting. There we pled our case.

Finally I said, "Now Chuck, if you'll stay here I'll make you the operations officer and promote you to major." Every man has his price. He bought the deal. He stayed.

Dick Ellis, John Henebry, Chuck Howe and Doc Gilmore in front of "Seabiscuit"

The successes we were having as an air power, the experiences I was living through and my personal accomplishments were satisfying enough to keep me flying combat. Even deaths like Wilkins' didn't cow me into considering rotation. I liked to fly. I liked to fight. Our armaments were good and getting better. We were on the offensive now. We were winning.

It was the best hunting I had ever had since my Uncle Charlie had me at age seven shooting at rabbits running through the prairie. The Air Corp perfected my style.

I enjoyed being the senior guy, in command of people and maneuvers. I worked well with those superior to me and they never suggested I go home. Air war challenged and fulfilled my expectations. I flew 219 missions before I was pulled from the front lines. I was still alive.

Twenty-five year olds in positions of command, even those with the secret trepidation I was experiencing, can make a go of it with the cooperation and confidence of the significant members of Group staff—including enlisted and noncom members in positions to contribute to the success of our missions. From the beginning of my military career I worked for and with men with more experience than I had and I learned all I could from them.

One major source of support for me was our group flight surgeon, John Gilmore. "Doc," serving the Third, was continuing a friendship we had begun the year before when he was the flight surgeon of the Ninetieth Squadron.

Doc, as flight surgeon serving through four commanders, knew all the old timers and all their secrets.

Surgeons, like chaplains, by virtue of their duties, were privy to delicate data. Non-judgmental in their approach, doctors were on the listening end with GIs and on up through the ranks. They could know the make-up of the entire organization better than any other level of officer. As medical men they could assess the mental stamina of the men in their care—how they were bearing the psychic shock of getting shot at almost daily. Kenney, Whitehead, Davies, those at the top of the military hierarchy used Gilmore and their other surgeons as reference sources when they needed reliable information about the physical and mental state of any of their men.

Doc sensed what the top brass required to command their airmen effectively. It was no doubt Gilmore who spread the word upstairs of my air adventures, particularly at Rabaul.

As I moved up through the ranks of Squadron Commander, Group Operations Officer and now Group Commanding Officer, I also depended upon the advice and counsel of this seasoned officer, only three years my senior, and the skeletons he kept in the chambers of his brain.

Doc Gilmore (left) with General Kenney

It was Doc Gilmore who first indicated my promotion to Group Commander when mid-November he returned from Fifth Bomber Command at Port Moresby telling me that Colonel Jim Davies was concerned about the spirit of the Third. Doc's advice to him was that it needed a commander equal to the rotated D. P. Hall, recommending me. So a few days later when the call came over the land line to meet with Davies at headquarters I was ready, made the appointment for that afternoon, cranked up my B-25 and flew over the Owen Stanley Range to keep it.

The meeting went well. So well that two days later I received orders by wire appointing me Group Commander of the Third Attack Group now followed by this promotion to lieutenant colonel.

A kid from the prairie, I ended up Pacific Theater duties having my name submitted for general, as was the name of my friend, Jimmy Stewart. I was 27 years old. Four days later, August 6, one plane dropped one bomb on Hiroshima, destroying Japan's will to make war, and all promotions were temporarily halted—including Jimmy's and mine. So went my chances of reaching stars before 30. Finally in 1948, as I turned 30 and by then in the reserves, I was promoted—along with Jimmy Stewart. It took us three more years but we did become generals together.

Advancing the Bomb Line

"The art of war is simple enough," advises Ulysses S. Grant. "Find out where your enemy is. Get at him as soon as you can. Strike at him as hard as you can, and keep moving on."

From GHQ, from MacArthur's mouth, was our modern day adaption: Advance the bomb line. Move it north! And with those orders we all moved—the Army, Halsey's Navy forces, the Australian ground troops under General Sir Thomas Blamey, Bill "Bull" Garing's Australian air forces and our Army Air directed by Kenney.

When the Australian and Yank ground troops secured Buna and Gona, the victories dramatically marked the beginning of the Bomb Line Advance. Here the specialized U.S. Army paratroopers made their first appearance in our theater, staging a drop supporting the Australian "diggers."

We were confidently relocated at Dobodura.

The Army, with the aerial support of our A-20Gs, was following up on the Marine's 1943 Christmas landing at Arawe with a major amphibious onslaught near Cape Gloucester at New Britain's northwest tip.

Finschhafen on the eastern tip of New Guinea's Huon peninsula was on the brink of recapture.

Australians and Yanks in lock step were marching up the north coast of New Guinea having recovered Wau and Salamaua.

Nadzab and Lae fell.

Lae, with its garrison of anti-aircraft and maintenance personnel and its hand-picked fighter pilots, had been a prime target for the U.S. and the Aussie air forces since April 1942, three months before I joined the Third at Charters Towers with the gang from San Francisco. We had listened to an accumulation of three months of horror stories of some of the Pacific war's fiercest air battles exalting the superiority of Lae's seasoned planes and pilots.

The Third's few old A-20s and its few old dive-bombing A-24s originally had been no match for these Japanese fighter planes. The power of our daring P-39s and P-40s shrunk into shadows in skies populated by the experienced, proud and victorious Japanese pilots just arriving from their conquests in China and southeast Asia. The air was indisputably theirs. Lae unceasingly sent out its air support as escorts for Rabaul bombers to assault almost daily the critical Port Moresby area.

We became as persistent. Our planes nightly crawled around the mountains and began roaring down on them, skimming over the treetops, raining bombs and gunfire over the dirty little airfield. We fired at everything that moved. They hid their aircraft in tunnels in the mountains to spare them. By day we scoured the seas smashing at Japanese ships supplying them. We would starve them out.

Finally they withdrew to Wewak.

Now here I was, less than a year and a half later touching down on an airstrip that had been our constant target since my first days in combat. Here I was landing in territory that we had bombed and strafed unmercifully as recently as a few weeks ago, territory that had put up an equally vigorous defense. Lae, where so many of our comrades went down.

The airbase was secured. Runways that in more peaceful times had provided for airlifted supplies of gold ore to and from the productive Kakoda mines in the Owen Stanley Mountains were patched now for our use. Allied mechanization had reached such a degree of efficiency that construction was sure and fast.

I was finally taking a plane into Lae. It was my first landing on a former enemy base. Such a major base. The experience, the odd, sobering and satisfying experience brought the purpose of the war home. Winning is satisfying. In war, winning has no substitute.

It was clear that we were pushing the enemy home. They were fading into the jungles as we advanced, trying to work their way north and west where they expected salvation. But we had shut down their largest center of supply in the Pacific and were intercepting the occasional promising ships and coastal traffic along the north coast as far west as Wewak. The Japanese warrior was becoming a sorry sight, scattering before our advances, unsupplied and unsupported by his homeland.

During the entire war to this point I had seen only one captive Japanese, spotting him after that significant landing at Lae. A classic "sad sack," he was a pitiful sight. Emaciated, clothed in only a G-string, he appeared to be quite sick. Squatting on the ground, his legs were shackled but his hands were free. He was under the nonchalant care of a G.I. rifleman.

Rather than a Japanese soldier, more likely he was a laborer, one of the horde of captive labor units the Japanese moved along with their advances. Impressed laborers, finding less honor in their lot, were more willing to surrender alive than did the warriors to whom there was no greater disgrace than surrender.

With the concurrent capture and occupation of nearby Nadzab, an immediate construction of airstrips began, using lightweight airborne equipment flown in by C-47s. The Fifth Air Force was landing these loaded C-47s the same day the paratroopers were securing the village. In less than a week our A-20s and P-38 fighters were operating off newly constructed runways.

While Lae at least had boasted a hardtop runway, Nadzab had been nothing more than a native village with a grass airstrip before the Japanese occupation in January 1942. The two villages lay at the southeast end of the Markham River Valley, a 50 mile long stretch of kunai grass flatlands between 13,000 foot mountain ranges beginning at the Huon Gulf and forging northwest into the interior of Papua New Guinea. The valley floor is level and unforested. The kunai grass there is six to eight feet tall, very strong, almost impenetrable on foot. The soil in the Nadzab area, 18 miles up the valley and only a few feet above sea level, is coarse and gravelly. The Corps of Engineers found almost ideal conditions to construct an excellent multi-runway airdrome to serve us in our burgeoning push north and west.

New Guinea nationals teamed with the Army Corps of Engineers and Australians to create not only a major Allied base here but added a road traversing 18 miles of difficult jungle terrain to connect it with the seaport and airstrips at Lae.

View of Nadzab

144

Further, the friendly Australian administrators who policed and trained the young indigenous personnel organized work platoons to build our offices and living quarters, fashioned from poles and protected with completely waterproof thatched roofs. They rigged up a saw mill capable of turning out planks for tent flooring.

The Army engineers pulled a water tank from a wrecked truck and winced it up to the highest point above our camp site. Water ran through a system of pipes and hoses to each living area blessing each of us with running water for laundry and showers. We were ripe for the minimal comforts of home that Yank resourcefulness was finally able to provide.

The quarters I shared with two other group officers were built on a hill overlooking the airdrome. Beyond it was the spectacular valley. Our thatched roof overhung walls of woven bamboo panels. Inside, true to our native motif, our rooms were furnished sparsely, with Army issue cots and folding chairs.

We found there the most pleasant surroundings yet encountered on this island. In addition to its exquisite beauty, the Markham River Valley had less rainfall than we had grown accustomed to—meaning no swamps and few mosquitos.

Best of all, we had jumped 200 miles closer to the "Land of the Rising Sun."

The Third Attack Group bar, "The 3rd Slug Bar," became a famous place that even General Kenney and General Whitehead would visit with their senior officers.

At Nadzab, the Third Attack Group, displaying its Grim Reapers logo, was able to have all four squadrons (8th, 13th, 89th, 90th) based at the same airfield.

General Kenney was charged. In less than a month after capturing Nadzab he had us operating out of the largest airdrome complex in the Southwest Pacific with four black-top runways, dispersal taxiway and revetments operating A-20s, B-25s, P-38s, P-47 Thunderbolts, B-17s, B-24s and C-47s. For the first time since arriving in Australia, the Third Attack Group Headquarters and all four squadrons, the Eighth, Thirteenth, Eighty-Ninth and Ninetieth were a unified whole, based together in the same place at the same time.

To sweeten the scene, each squadron was equipped with 16 new, fresh-from-the-factory Douglas A-20Gs, 64 of the 96,000 military aircraft the U.S. produced that year. With this new aircraft, maintaining our in-commission rate at the standard 75 per cent combat ready would present no problem for our experienced, hardworking mechanical and ordnance personnel. Keeping 12 of each squadron's 16 planes ready to go at all times would only be a crunch were we to be assigned a maximum effort of several missions in a compressed period of a few days.

Finally came the call for this maximum effort. In February 1944 our orders were to neutralize the airstrips on the Admiralty Islands, about 50 miles north of our Nadzab base.

We first attacked the airfield at Los Negros, an island with a good harbor just off the eastern tip of the main Admiralty Island of Manus.

This maximum effort was against minimal defenses. Several wrecked aircraft and light and inaccurate anti-aircraft fire provided our only targets. The few aircraft we did strafe would not burn. They were out of fuel. Obviously, the Japanese had moved out. A few abandoned fighters were left to protect nothing with nothing.

We continued to stay after their shipping off the north coast beyond Wewak. The targets were dwindling to a few motor launches and barges.

The nature of war was changing as the enemy fled. One morning in January 1944 we were assigned the unpleasant task of annihilating a herd of cattle grazing on the coastal plain between Finschhafen and Saidor. With the Japanese chased out of Finschhafen and Lae and moving northwest by foot, they had no dependable home support. They were living off the land. We tore up their crops wherever we spotted cultivated fields. The target cattle were in their path and could have provided a feast for their run. Destroying them, strafing them by air, would deny the enemy fresh meat for their flight. Without preservation, the destroyed cattle would be edible for about a day maximum before the tropical climate rotted the carcasses.

We searched the non-wooded plains in three A-20s, found herd of some 30 head and completed the nasty job.

It gave me the same queasy feeling I had experienced when a kennel of dogs was a target. In their efforts to secure what territory they held in the Rabaul area, the Japanese had created a team of police dogs expertly trained to give the alarm and even attack and hold intruders. The Australian ground troops were often their prey. Death or imprisonment was often the result.

The Australians had pinpointed the kennels and asked if I could bomb them. I could and did, bringing all my combat expertise to the mission but without any of the enthusiasm I brought to destroying enemy airdromes and shipping.

How low can a low altitude strafer go?

Continuing up the coast toward Saidor on a nobler search and destroy hunt we neared what we thought was an abandoned airstrip. We spotted an anti-aircraft gun position that we decided to neutralize. It was sitting out in the open, an inviting target. We had some parafrag bombs on board that we could drop inside the surrounding sandbags, polishing it off. At minimum altitude I started a strafing attack.

At the onset of the run, I was within less than a mile of the target when two Japanese soldiers came running out of the bushes on my left, moving toward the gun position. The moving targets were almost a full deflection shot at 90 degrees to my left.

Three short burst from the fifties downed them. Neither made it to the gun position. They went ass over appetite for the emperor. And that was that. Great hunting with an easy target.

Having nearly reached our useful range for the day with no extra fuel tanks on board, we turned back south to climb over the Finisterre Range to our new home at Nadzab.

In the quiet of the flight back, the killing of the herd of helpless cattle troubled me. But that uneasiness was balanced by the satisfying feeling of taking out the gunners. Was I nuts? Mourning the demise of cattle while celebrating the death of humans?

Is the difference the intent? Those Japanese were scurrying to bring me down. Firing on them preserved my life. The peacefully grazing cattle had no belligerent purpose at all. Unfortunately, their use as food to an evil, fleeing enemy predetermined their fate. We wasted them. Waste is a part of war.

18

Island Villages

I was knowingly disobeying a military order, but I held my fire.

The fleeing enemy, 100,000-strong, without the possibility of a sea escape, moved northwest by foot with no food, no medicine, little ammunition, no leadership over a route that included jungles, mountains, insects, equatorial heat and our constant harassment.

We would rarely see the Japanese from the air but information on their routes was abundant and accurate. So we knew they were primarily following the coastline where traveling was easier.

Thus, Fifth Bomber Command issued orders to search and destroy along these coastal routes above Madang as far north as Wewak. Strafe everything that moved. The command was based on intelligence that Papuan nationals along the route were assisting the beginnings of a Japanese evacuation of the Huon Peninsula.

The search and destroy targets included local villages.

Never before had we had such inclusive distasteful orders. Our familiarity with the ways of the nationals gave us reason to doubt the equity of blanket strafing. We all knew stories of brave Papuan resistance to the Japanese invaders, made more effective by the military training many had received from ANGAU. Their contributions on behalf of the war effort were widespread, heroic and important.

Perhaps some able bodies had been pressed into service by the Japanese military as carriers, but unilateral voluntary cooperation with the invaders was unknown.

With this relationship in mind but with orders in hand we set out along our route and came suddenly upon the first village, completely surprising its inhabitants. People were standing in the open looking up at our low flying planes, by now used to our presence, trusting. I vividly remember the faces of the women and children. I also remember an old man sensing danger, trying to run from us with the aid of a long walking stick. This was not the enemy.

I could not strafe. We would stand guilty of not obeying orders and I was content with that decision.

We moved beyond the village up the coast to well below Wewak, never seeing any sign of a fleeing enemy. The Japanese were not moving in the open during the daytime hours. cover was abundant. Roads were scarce.

We came across now many local villages but having made the decision not to strafe, we let them be.

When our three A-20s returned to Nadzab from the mission, I immediately took my Jeep the few miles down the road to Fifth Bomber Command. I needed to talk immediately with the officers in operations about the futility of strafing the villages, the injustice of killing a population that provided no evidence of helping the enemy. These innocent people were trying to exist on their own soil in spite of a foreign invasion brought about through no fault of their own. No more. The only use the enemy could have made of them would have been to put their healthy young men out as carriers. Those staying in the villages had little to offer the war effort.

Brigadier General James Crabb, the commander of Bomber Command, seemed to agree and offered to take the matter up to Fifth Air Force. By the next day the orders had changed. We were to leave the villages untouched.

The Japanese had been hard enough on the Papuans, beating them and ravaging their homes. It made us happy to have our planes in the air bring them some hope of peace.

There were times when our planes meant more than peace to the Papuans. After we had settled into the Mount Hagen area a delegation of local warriors, representing, said their chief, some 500 spearmen and bowmen, brought their war plans against a neighboring tribe to us. They wanted air support.

These neighbors had raided their village some months previous stealing away with untold numbers of pigs and women, two precious commodities in the jungle. The chief emotionally proclaimed his pro-American sympathies and assumed his enemy was our enemy. Cooperation with air cover for his spear and bow attack would not come without compensation, he promised. He was perfectly willing to split the booty—the enemy's women and pigs he would capture in retribution.

True, we hadn't had a more intriguing offer or more enticing rewards from General MacArthur, but we delicately declined the proposed mission and encouraged continued camaraderie with a formal pig roast and native dance in exchange for our gifts of costume jewelry, gold-lipped shells and tobacco. The chief decided to forego combat if it weren't to be backed with U.S. air power.

One of the chiefs and his contingent from the jungle surrounding the Third Attack Group

One Lucky Fellow

Aᴛᴛᴇʀ several weeks without any Japanese air opposition, we came upon a small freighter off the coast of Wewak that provided the only type of challenge the current war was offering. Small pickings.

We sunk it.

We had finished a second run on the freighter when I saw a yellow dab in the blue sea. Turning my A-20 back for a close-up look, I verified what I had originally suspected—a Yank in a yellow life vest. Fortunately for both of us the Japanese were mounting no air opposition. The Yank and we had the sea and the sky to ourselves.

On the way back to Nadzab I raised our new, innovative and welcomed rescue service using flying boats capable of 120 mph speeds. Prior to the initiation of the Army Air rescue squadrons, a flier down at sea, no matter what service, once sighted and reported depended on Navy planes, surface vessels and submarines searching and rescuing.

The Australians had instituted a reconnaissance and recovery system similar to ours before our entry into the war. Their specially trained crews operated the venerable PBY, a seaplane. They covered their war zone through 24 hour missions.

I reported the location of the sighting. Because of the lateness of the day, the rescue team was unable to find the lone survivor until the next morning. By that time I knew he was one of our own A-20 pilots who had hit the mast of the transport, damaging the plane so badly that he had to ditch in the water.

The rear gunner on the plane was lost but the pilot had extricated himself and floated in his life vest through the night until finally recovered at daybreak.

One lucky fellow—although he had lost his gunner and his A-20 he had been sighted and rescued from the vast sea.

Our man was twice lucky. Bad luck in the air battle. Good luck in the sea.

He was one of some 2,000 plucked from the waters from the summer of 1943 when the system was inaugurated and continued to the end of the war. These were the men who, in addition to good luck, were flying planes equipped with parachutes, flares, life preservers, life rafts, special rations and medical supplies—any one of which could decide life or death. These were the men who maintained the coolness to apply the survival skills they had been taught, had weather conditions on their side, were flying planes that ditched well and were known to have bailed out or forced a landing at sea. The quickness of the arrival of the rescue team and the equipment it carried increased a downed flier's chances of survival. A pilot in trouble kept in mind any edge he had to continually weigh his chances of survival as his luck played out.

Third Attack Group A-20G skip bombing a freighter near New Guinea, actually hitting the mast of the ship, which caused the pilot to ditch the plane.

The DSC

THE Distinguished Service Cross has been awarded since 1918 by the Army to any in its ranks for exceptional heroism in combat. It is a bronze eagle affixed to an embellished cross. It was the second military decoration established by Congress and is the second highest award created, second only to the Congressional Medal of Honor.

One morning operations at Seventeen-Mile advised me that a major general, an infantry officer on MacArthur's staff, was arriving from GHQ to make a flight over New Guinea's north coast with me. We had been flying reconnaissance for some time and we did not anticipate any enemy encounters.

The general was delivered to my plane, occupied the copilot seat and we proceeded on our three and a half hour flight across the Owen Stanley Range, up the north coast, past Salamaua, up to Lae, back across the mountains and down to the Seventeen-Mile airstrip at Port Moresby.

During the flight the general talked little. I felt he was uncomfortable in this aviation environment. When we landed he said, "Good bye and thank you very much," moved to a Jeep and departed.

A few weeks after that particularly undistinguished flight I met Phil R. North, a Notre Dame buddy from Fort Worth, Texas now on the GHQ staff. He congratulated me on my decoration.

"Decoration?"

"The Distinguished Service Cross."

"I haven't been awarded any Distinguished Service Cross—or anything to compare with it."

"Well, General Frank received one."

"General Frank?"

"The officer from GHQ that you took on a reconnaissance flight last month. I assumed you were awarded the DSC along with him."

John Henebry, Bill Dunn (CBS reporter), Phil North and Doc Gilmore
photographed in front of "Queen Mary" in 1945.

Not so. It was a routine flight, not deserving of any awards. We had been in control of the air over that particular territory since the autumn of 1943.

The Distinguished Service Cross is awarded by Headquarters, the recipient recommended by staff. It hangs impressively on the chest, and it has a well-established place in the military. But, it can be vulnerable to office politics.

21

Hollandia

WE were running out of targets. By March 1944 every enemy airfield in Papua New Guinea that we had pounded so relentlessly over the past two years had been captured, neutralized or bypassed. Even Wewak was winding down. We had not had a report on any aircraft activity in the area for some time.

The Japanese original threatening thrust into the Southwest Pacific was withering for lack of their ability to resupply as we grew in power. Their movement now was north and west in withdrawal. Rabaul, the major air base and harbor, was "dying on the vine," no longer the vital destination for ships and planes coming from the home islands and from Truk. We used it for bombing practice for our new replacements. Our Navy and Army Air, knocking out the significant bases, had neutralized the supply routes.

We attacked the now-and-then shipping moving off New Guinea's north coast as we pushed the bomb line up and out, following the fleeing enemy. We were looking to the Philippines, a long shot from our current base at Nadzab. Between here and there remained a lot of real estate and a lot of Japanese.

Closer—some 525 miles west and a little north at Humboldt Bay—was Hollandia right beyond the Dutch New Guinea border. It was the next significant Japanese base still in operation with 400 warplanes at the ready. Hollandia was about two degrees south of the equator. This war was hot and getting hotter as we pursued the enemy north.

Five hundred and twenty five miles was a stretch for our A-20Gs scheduled to carry a full load of fuel, bombs, ammunition and crew of three. The challenge prompted Major General Ennis C. Whitehead to call a meeting at Nadzab, now his Advanced Fifth Air Force Headquarters. Brigadier Generals Jimmy Crabb, the commander of Fifth Bomber Command, and Paul "Squeeze" Wurtsmith, the commander of Fifth Fighter Command, came in. As did many of Fifth Air Force's staff members, including then Colonel, later Brigadier General, Merion C. Cooper, Whitehead's chief of staff.

Normally a serious, strict and effective commander, Whitehead on this day was in a rather expansive mood. He had been in charge of Kenney's day-to-day operations out of Port Moresby since July 1942, freeing Kenney to attend to Army Air business at MacArthur's Australian headquarters, a continual reminder to the Supreme Commander and his ground-pounding staff that the Army Air was in the war to stay and win.

Whitehead had just received from the enemy camp what he considered the most monumental compliment a Yank could hear. Because of the effectiveness of his air defense, especially because of his relentless air strikes, Tokyo Rose, the American enemy propaganda broadcaster later convicted of treason, decried that this "heartless American air commander," calling him by name, "was breaking all the rules of warfare against the Japanese." She labeled him "Ennis the Menace, the Murderer of Moresby."

He cherished it. He made great sport of it as he opened the meeting to warn the troops what a despicable person was our boss. He explained that Tokyo Rose was particularly angry at his annihilation of the Japanese stronghold at Rabaul where by night his heavy bombers had been dropping thousand pound bombs with the newly developed proximity fuses set to explode a couple of hundred feet above ground. She resented the damage and confusion.

"What the hell does she think war is all about?" Whitehead growled through his guttural laugh. "Wait until we finish Hollandia," he added. "She will have plenty more to complain about. I wonder if she'll invent a new name for me then."

That was our introduction to Hollandia, followed by Whitehead's concern over the great distance between us and the three target air strips there. He wanted the attack to involve fighter cover and heavy bombers, followed by his three "knock 'em dead" groups comprising 12 squadrons of strafers. He envisioned 96 B-25s and 48 A-20s flying on the deck at 50 to 100 feet, strafing and dropping their 23-pound parafraq "daisy cutter" bombs.

The couple dozen of us were agreeing enthusiastically with Whitehead's scheme as he asked for any comments.

Colonel Cooper had a contribution.

A Georgia boy, Cooper had been with Fifth Air Force Headquarters since the early Port Moresby days and knew the theater and the enemy well. His background and experiences were vast. He had been friends with General George Kenney since World War I flying school days, a friendship that continued in France through that war.

In addition to the considerable combat flying experience he had gathered, with the defeat of the Germans, he had joined the Polish Air Force, flying against the Russian Communists. Shot down in unfriendly territory, the Soviets held him prisoner until he finally escaped and found his way back to Poland.

He next emerged in the motion picture industry as a Hollywood writer, director and producer. In the early thirties he became head of the financially troubled RKO Studios, pulling it into the black with a series of successful movies including "Grass," the first major documentary shot on location, "Flying Down to Rio," "Quiet Man," "Last Days of Pompeii," "This is Cinerama" and "King Kong." His weapons were such legendaries as Gary Cooper, Fred Astaire whom he wooed away from Broadway, Ginger Rogers, Katherine Hepburn and John Ford.

This new glitter-life was as extraordinary as his former warrior's life. Throughout his careers, he saw all the tall buildings.

During those glamorous days after WWI he maintained his connection with Generals Kenney and Whitehead. When WWII broke out, like many of his fellow WWI fire horses, he was compelled to get back into harness. We first timers called them "retreads." "Coop" came from the China Air Task Force and was an eagle colonel by the time he wound up in New Guinea in 1943 as Ennis the Menace's Chief of Staff.

As a strategist, Cooper was legendary. It was he who designed a Saturday night attack on a Rabaul whore house earlier in the war after putting ashore marines to identify the primary destination of off-duty Japanese officers.

An inveterate pipe smoker, Coop had the burner at hand constantly. When he wasn't puffing, he was refilling his pipe, packing it, lighting it. Nursing his pipe bowl as ideas on how best to strike Hollandia flew about, Coop eventually had to make his contribution.

Pipe in hand, he approached the large wall map in the Fifth Air Force war room to detail his considered plan with the help of his pipe as pointer.

Well into his presentation, the center of planned attack began moving higher than his pipe stem was long. The pipe stem was missing effective focuses so Whitehead supplied a substitute pointer and the discussion proceeded. Coop was an intense guy, who once into his delivery, was not easily disturbed. He accepted the pointer and put his pipe away.

Growing along with Coop's excitement about his plan was a slight distracting rumble. Smoke was coming out of the hip pocket of his khaki trousers. But he remained intense, engrossed in expressing his thoughts on the pivotal strike. Rather than stopping his stream of thought to pull his pipe out of his pocket, he repeatedly slapped his rear end and continued layering idea upon idea.

The murmurs from his audience became more pronounced, but that didn't break Coop's concentration. He was peaking when finally General Whitehead yelped "Coop, your ass is on fire. If you put out the embers, we might better be able to follow what you're talking about."

It had become obvious to everyone in the room that Coop was so consumed by his own strategies that his unconsciously stuffed pipe burning away his hip pocket wasn't on his agenda at all.

Surprisingly enough, a plan for striking Hollandia was formulated out of that raucous afternoon.

Whitehead's heavy B-24 bombers with P-38 fighter cover were to attack first from 20,000 feet dropping fragmentation bombs.

The morning after the B-24 strike, assigned to hit whatever was left, would be 144 low level strafers and bombers gathered into three groups of A-20s and B-25s from the Eighth, Thirteenth, Eighty-Ninth and Ninetieth Squadrons of the Third Attack Group with the Thirty-Eighth and 345th Groups.

Taking into consideration the requirements of the mission, including the details of the approach, the individual target assignments and the departure from the target, the speed differential of our planes put the Third in front. And thus it fell upon me to lead the entire morning-after mission—a mission that was so successful that Whitehead awarded me the Distinguished Flying Cross in appreciation of the efforts of the airmen.

To minimize the problem that the 525 one-way miles from Nadzab presented, Whitehead decided that the A-20s should take off early and stage through Gusap, 75 miles up the Markham Valley, and top off the fuel tanks there, shortening the long run to Hollandia.

That was the plan we followed that morning, April 3, 1944, as we of the Third arrived and found the fuel service personnel at Gusap ready and waiting. When all 48 A-20s were refilled we signaled Nadzab to launch the 96 B-25s of the waiting eight squadrons. In formation they got on course for Gusap while we, in a few more minutes, started launching and forming up. As the first of the B-25s was sighted approaching Gusap we took up the lead in our A-20s, on course into Dutch New Guinea, our first penetration into that neighboring half of the island.

We flew westerly up the Markham Valley, over the Ramu River, over 200 miles of swamp and alligators, and across the famous Sepik River, inland about 50 miles from Wewak. Now we were accomplishing one of the famous MacArthur bypasses—letting another stronghold "die on the vine."

Two hundred and forty miles beyond Wewak we were abeam of Mount Cyclops, rising more than 7,000 feet immediately north of Lake Sentani and the neighboring airfields, our primary Hollandia targets.

Mount Cyclops was a distinct landmark. Our plan of approach to the target area was to stay inland, past Cyclops and Lake Sentani, staying south and very low, thus avoiding detection. At a point 25 miles beyond, making a low level right turn would put us in line with our objectives. The absolutely clear day enabled us to keep the mountain constantly in view.

The plan was flawless. A few minutes after making our prescribed right swing, Mount Cyclops now coming up on our left, we came out right on target.

What a beautiful target—the Sentani airfields were at the base of a peninsula wedged between the immense Lake Sentani and the sharply rising Mount Cyclops. A memorable, picturesque sight.

It worked. We got in on them by surprise. Our first target, spotted in reconnaissance photos, was to have been antiaircraft guns positioned on a ridge above the airfields. We saw nothing until we were half way through the target. What fire there was then was light and inaccurate. Three airplanes on the left of our formation were assigned to neutralizing that minimal anti-aircraft artillery.

Some ground vehicles were moving about. Particularly appealing was a gas truck directly in front of me that a couple of squirts from my six fifty-calibers brought to a stop. As it started burning, two men jumped out of the cab and fell flat to the ground. Playing dead or hit? I'll never know.

The meat of the target was rows of planes lined up at varying angles, hundreds of single and twin engine planes. Some were parked in dirt revetments and some unprotected in the open. Many were wrecked from the high level bomber raid the day before but some had been left undamaged. This is what we had come for, our targets of opportunity—this and whatever useful equipment we could find to destroy.

We also were loaded with parafrag bombs. Attacking the targets from west to east at low altitude, we strafed and bombed through the entire airdrome area. Twelve formations, 12 planes each flying abreast, our 144 planes gave the "sons of heaven" a working over. We left them in total devastation, an aerial fleet reduced to rubble.

We saw no Japanese fighter plane opposition until we were through the airdrome complex. Hollandia was considered to be outside our range. I was starting a slight climb to clear the comparatively low hills to the east of Lake Sentani. One single engine plane, off to my left at quite a distance, was moving away.

Then unexpectedly I sighted a single engine fighter at about half a mile from and slightly above me, crossing my line of flight, moving from my right to my left. I pushed both throttles full forward for full power and continued a slight climb to close in on him.

Still at a distance, as I fired one burst of my machine guns, something dropped from the enemy plane. From my position it looked like two sticks several feet long tied together by a rope or cable falling 20 or 30 feet apart and directly before me. My gunner in the rear gun turret saw it also but couldn't identify it.

I swerved to clear whatever it was for fear it would catch on a wing or prop, or it might be explosive.

An unusual coincidence or a clever defensive mechanism? Neither of us could determine. We had an observer on board with a camera poised for battle shots but he missed this shot and our only opportunity to identify it later.

If it were intended to be a defensive maneuver, it worked. While it didn't hit us nor cause damage to the plane, we did swerve allowing the Japanese pilot to escape by diving away.

Back on course we returned flying the remainder of the distance from

Hollandia. We had not encountered air opposition from Madang or Wewak on our way to the target earlier and expected none now. There was none. The weather was excellent with but a few high scattered clouds over the highest mountain peaks. Visibility was unlimited. The return was comfortable; we knew the Sepik and Ramu Rivers and Markham Valley routes well because of our many forays to the primary north coast targets, Wewak and Madang.

Again, our four squadrons of A-20s put into Gusap to top off with fuel and proceed the remaining 75 miles to Nadzab. As we refueled, the eight squadrons of B-25s landed back at our Nadzab home base.

It was 6 p.m., 12 fatiguing hours after take-off for our longest and largest combat mission since we first had arrived on New Guinea. For each of us in the A-20s, it was three takeoffs and three landings, two refuelings and six hours and 35 minutes of actual flying time for our deepest penetration into enemy territory. We didn't lose one of our 144 low-level strafers. We had painted the target with thousands of rounds of fifty-calibers and parafrag bombs. Whatever opposition the previous day's heavy B-24 bomber strike left, we nullified. Three hundred and forty planes were destroyed on the ground.

What did we confirm during that long day? That the Japanese were on the run. Our follow-up photos displayed wrecked planes that had not burned— obviously planes low on or out of fuel. After these two days of battle, Hollandia was no longer a hot target.

Enemy supply was a sorry situation and likely to remain so. Japanese were now low on all that was needed to wage the war they had begun. We gave them no hope of a reversal. Supply lines from the home islands to Japanese forces in the field were steadily, foray by foray, breaking down.

Wewak Again

THE Japanese weren't replenishing Wewak. Since our August 17, 1943, Borum wipe-out strike—the first, the greatest, the most devastating strike against the four Wewak airstrips—Yank and Aussie strafers, medium bombers and high level heavy bombers had been discouraging another buildup.

Eventually we began to bypass Wewak for juicier targets. We considered it neutralized. Two days prior we had flown the Wewak area and found nothing to shoot at but a small freighter at sea, some 25 miles south and east. Saw it and sank it with no Wewak-based aerial opposition.

Still, headquarters laid on a strike by two of our squadrons. It would involve 24 A-20s hitting the main airstrip, Borum, again. We wondered why, but we mounted our beasts and charged.

Seven-thirty the morning of the strike, the weather was good, CAVU. We took off early from the flatgrass plains of Nadzab and formed up en route into two squadron formations of three-ship Vs, proceeding northwest up the Markham River Valley. Flying at a comfortable altitude of about 2,000 feet in the calm of the early morning quiet. No turbulence. No air masses bumping into each other. Cool air coming in through the cockpit air vents, cool for that neighborhood, only six degrees south of the equator where hotter than hell is the norm. The sun was rising directly at our backs. All around us was a beautiful, peaceful sight.

Below us was the lush green valley where the Ramu and Markham Rivers are fed by white water streams draining thousands of feet down mountains on either side. Northwest was the expansive and treacherous Sepik River flowing into the Bismarck Sea.

A fascinating non-combative advantage of low level attack aviation was seeing close-up what I was flying over. It made the plane and the land part of me. High altitude flight has its place in war but it is a much different and more memorable experience to be able to count the coconuts.

We flew along the Markham River and over Gusap. The recently captured airstrip was now serving P-38 fighters as an alternate landing strip. Nearing the west end of the Markham Valley, we were coming abreast of Madang, some 40 miles north on the coast, a Japanese seaport and airfield. Time now to descend to less than 100 feet altitude to avoid detection while flying the next 160 miles along the Ramu and across the Sepik Rivers and adjacent swamps.

After almost 45 minutes of ground level swamp flying, we climbed to more than 1,500 feet to clear the jungle-covered beginnings of the low-slung Prince Alexander Range, the guardians of Wewak from the south. As we passed over their eastern tip, we started our descent, dipping as close to ground level as possible. We were hugging the tree tops again and tightened up our loose, long range formation in preparation for our minimum altitude strafing and bombing run on the principal and easternmost airstrip, hoping to maintain what little surprise element we might have had as our only possible defense.

Because of the target's coastal location, with the Pacific Ocean to the north and the Alexander Range up tight immediately to the south, because of so many recent, debilitating strikes, the chance anymore of getting in on them by surprise was minimal to nonexistent. The Japanese now had radar and most probably a well developed system of spotters throughout the surrounding hills.

In spite of all this, here we were striking Borum once more anyway.

We hadn't spotted any Japanese air opposition and, now in sight of the airstrip, all remained quiet. Not yet in range to start firing our six fifty-calibers, we were fast closing on them—in formation at full throttle moving about 230 mph. Ahead of us were wrecks of aircraft and damaged equipment. Nothing in one working piece. Just as we had thought might be the case.

The Japanese had quit putting planes down at Borum. The airstrip personnel were stuck there still, lacking weapons, sick from malaria and dysentery. They escaped later by foot hoping for an occasional submarine or barge rescue.

As we were getting the airstrip into our range, their ground defenses started firing, light and inaccurate. Unconcerned, we continued on down the airstrip strafing and dropping our 23 lb. parafrag bombs. Still nothing moved.

Naturally, I began to wonder what in the hell I was doing here over a dissipated target with nothing of military value to shoot at. During this wonder-stricken moment, I got hit. Where on my A-20 and by what kind of ground fire I couldn't tell. All I knew was it was something positive, sudden and noisy, a straight-away thud.

We continued traveling the length of the strip on the deck and started a left turn to put us out of danger, out of range of additional ground fire. We eventually headed southeasterly and home. I checked on the intercom with my rear gunner who reported himself and the ship "okay"—not able to see any damage from ground fire.

Both engines were running beautifully. Oil pressure, manifold pressure and rpm were all "in the green." There was no vibration and the plane was handling normally. Where was the hit? It is always possible to take a hit that causes little damage in a non-vital area. Was that our situation?

Just as we cleared the hills to the south and east of the target my rear gunner called on the intercom to "look at the right wing." I did, to see light trailing smoke. I looked more carefully trying to spot fire but could see no flames. All the gauges remained "in the green." We had all the symptoms of a hit somewhere on the right wing but I couldn't see the cause.

I had no choice but to set a course for the nearest friendly territory. Back just the way we came—another 160 miles across the dreaded Sepik and Ramu River swamps plus at least another 30 or so miles to get out of probable enemy territory.

Everything still running well. If the wing didn't blow up or disintegrate we would make it to dry and friendly terrain.

Major Dick Walker from our Eighth Squadron pulled alongside in his A-20 to communicate with us on our Group frequency. Other than a little smoke everything seemed to him to be in one piece. The news was slightly comforting but experience warned me that with this smoke somewhere there should be fire. Discomforting was the fact that we were still over Japanese territory, albeit rivers and swamps inhabited only by crocodiles, snakes and mosquitos.

What should I do? Stay at my low altitude of about 1,000 feet above this inhospitable neighborhood or gain the advantage of height in case we do lose the wing and need to bail out or be forced to land. Ideally, we would stay with the plane. It offered some protection from the elements and a possible means of communication. I would rather land in the swamp with a dinghy on my ass and a Mae West around my neck than parachute to the ground having sacrificed communication and a protective shell.

A little more altitude was the answer. At about 200 mph taking us away from danger I gradually climbed to 5,000 feet. On this route, I concluded it to be the only sensible choice I had.

The plane was still running well but I couldn't know how long it would hold out. All the gauges were still "in the green." We had plenty of fuel left. Our bomb load had been dropped. We were light and were able to cruise at about 225. If we could make it at least to dry land and better yet—to Gusap.

Another problem! Rather the same problem but more of it. More smoke pouring out from the right wing, now from between the panels of the several wing sections. Everything else continued running well.

I could see two major mountain ranges in the distance. On the left going up to more than 13,000 feet was the Finisterre Range and a little closer on the right was the Bismarck Range rising to nearly 15,000 feet. Right between them was the very inviting Markham River Valley , 15 to 25 miles wide for a stretch of 95 miles. If I could get to the western opening of that valley we would at least be able to bail out or crash on dry, friendly land. If our plane would keep running as well as it had been, if it didn't burst into flames, we would meet the ground on our terms.

That expansive Markham Valley now had an allure beyond its exuberant beauty. We were still chugging away on a perfectly clear day, now just past the middle of the morning. With the floor of the valley 4,900 feet below us, we could see a long way.

Finally entering the valley, I suddenly realized that I had seen all the rivers, swamp and jungles with their lofty trees dripping with mosses that I ever wanted to see at close range and that dry land ahead was very inviting.

Now 180 miles removed from our morning target, we had at least made our first objective—to escape enemy territory. We were still 125 miles from our home base at Nadzab, but Gusap was only half that distance from our present position. I decided to put in there and not stretch our luck, having already used up more than our share.

Gusap was right in the center of the valley. We had earlier flown over it. It should be easy to locate but I was straining my eager eyes to find it. All of a sudden right before me, a pilot with an airplane on fire, was one of life's most beautiful surprises—an airstrip dead ahead. It couldn't have been Gusap this close to the mouth of the valley. Not Gusap, but the remains of a former missionary strip some 3,000 feet long, level and grassy. The good Lord must have placed it there just for us. It had no other current purpose on this war-ravaged land. Its name, I later discovered, was Dumpu.

Without hesitation I dropped the landing gear and flaps and thanked Him. I now had "three in the green"—all three gears down and locked. I throttled all the way back and proceeded straight in, landing without incident. I cleared the runway and climbed out. My rear gunner was already out. Walker, who had escorted us all the way across the mighty Sepik in his A-20, circled once and landed. The right wing was still smoking, now minimally. Still no visible fire.

Centered in the leading edge of the wing was a hole that looked to be about the size of a 20 millimeter shell. Without tools we couldn't examine the interior of the wing, but we figured the oil tank at the top of the wing behind the right engine nacelle was hit. The wing was hot—too hot to touch— hot all the way out to the tip.

After a few minutes the smoke subsided. Then all we could do was close up the plane, tie it down, put on the external control locks and climb into Walker's A-20 to proceed on down the Markham, past Gusap to Nadzab.

Our home base was only 85 miles from Dumpu. We immediately organized a mechanical maintenance crew under the direction of Major John Robinson, group engineering officer. His men flew back to Dumpu to assess the damage and prepare the plane for flight back to Nadzab for repair. I joined them the next day.

The repair crew found that the oil reservoir self-sealing tank had been hit either by an incendiary shell or an armor-piercing tracer. It had entered the leading edge of the wing striking the tank. Instead of flaming, the self-sealing tank smoldered, fed with enough ram air forced through the comparatively small shell hole, less than two inches. When the air stopped ramming through the hole, the lack of oxygen extinguished the smoldering unit.

Ram air is air that normally is forced through a duct by the speed of the aircraft, cooling the engines, bringing welcomed air into the cockpit. Ideally the function is under the pilot's control. The unexpected ram air we were contending with here was potentially lethal.

When the crew opened the wing panel above the oil reservoir it found that the entire top of the rubberized self-sealing tank had totally burned off in flight. Only our landing had halted the supply of air ramming through the shell hole, circulating inside the wing around the tank.

How much longer we could have flown with the smoldering oil we will never know. With the appearance of Dumpu, we didn't need to find out. Had it been the gas tank, also contained within the wing, the scenario would have been more gruesome. Oil is not as volatile as airplane gas with its considerably lower flash point. How's that for luck?

As a temporary repair, the crew tied off the damaged oil tank and rigged a supply of oil from the left engine oil tank. At last I flew my plane back to Nadzab where a new oil tank was installed. Repaired and reinspected, the A-20 soon was put back on the track like a prized race horse.

Why had two of the premier squadrons of the Third flown this mission to Wewak with no serviceable Japanese aircraft on its airstrips? Following my return to Nadzab with my injured plane, I questioned the Fifth Bomber Command on the purpose of taking the risks that running at nothing but gun positions involved. What was the justification? The next day from Lieutenant General Ennis Whitehead's headquarters came the word that the operations and planning people heard and understood our concern. Their promise: no more strikes unless aerial reconnaissance or Coast Watchers information could verify targets worthy of the dangers.

Sentani

O N May 4, 1944, one month after the initial Hollandia strike, a flight of three A-20Gs landed on the Sentani Airfield at Hollandia, Dutch New Guinea to have a look at what was now ours. PCS (Permanent Change of Station) orders were in the making to move our Third Attack Group up.

The Army ground-pounders were "cleaning up the neighborhood." Amphibious landings on the beaches at Aitape, at Humboldt Bay, south of the airfields, and at Tanahmerah Bay, to the north, had brought in the infantry against light opposition. The Japanese were clearing out as fast as we were moving in.

The most recent reports were that there was no organized enemy left in the area. Japanese supply routes by this time were so severed their land troops were drying up. Independently, out of desperation they were abandoning the areas they had held. Our ground forces were aggressively encouraging them.

What numbers remained of these forces were forsaken by their war lords. Alone and unsupplied on a tropical island, was there another choice but desertion open to these sundered troops? Not in this war.

Soldiers who greeted us at Sentani Airfield were jubilant. Their landings had been easy—the easiest of the whole string of invasions through the Admiralty Islands and up the north coast of Papua New Guinea. They had yarns to tell and captured souvenirs to show. They were loaded down with swords, caps and flags, so many they willingly shared with us. I received a white flag with the big red Japanese roundel in the center, covered with Japanese signatures.

Our prized souvenirs were the 300-plus damaged Japanese planes scattered over the landscape, left behind.

The Sentani area was beautiful to behold framed by the nearby hills, the towering mountains in the distance and the lake waters glittering in the equatorial sun. All, of course, seen through the haze of rising dust from the Army engineer bulldozers pushing wrecked enemy aircraft aside and laying the foundations for new roads and runways.

By the end of May our Group, along with other outfits, had moved up from Nadzab and were well settled into our new campsite on the side of a hill overlooking the airstrips and the lake beyond.

The bomb line had made its longest jump in the war, 525 miles west and north from Nadzab, chasing Japanese who were pulling back toward the Philippines and away from their early conquests. Barely into Dutch New Guinea but out of Papua New Guinea, there was not much left for us to oppose on this outcrop of land that had been our disputed home since 1942.

From Sentani we took stabs at nearby pockets of enemy activity—Babo, Kokas, Boela. During a mission to Manokwari Harbor and its airstrip, we made a pass through the harbor. Nothing there.

On the way home we diverted to the Noemfoer Island airstrip with our bombs and ammunition still intact and surprised some Japanese crews working on a few planes and moving around the airstrip in trucks. Without a workable warning system the first awareness they had of us was when we started shooting at them and their equipment. The planes didn't burn, clearly out of fuel.

Serious opposition erupted spottily. Ground and air forces met tough fighting at Wakde Island, west of Hollandia, while trying to install communication facilities in territory populated by Japanese marines.

The strongest opposition MacArthur's ground forces met was making an amphibious landing at Biak, an island located 325 miles west of Hollandia and 50 miles east of Manokwari.

If ever was a candidate for a bypass, Biak was it. Japanese holding down the island were well armed with artillery pieces hidden in the hills overlooking the coastal plain inside the landing beaches. The ground fighting was surprisingly tough and we were called upon to fly several air support missions to knock out big Japanese guns that were pinning down attacking U.S. ground troops. The infantry eventually took the island after a more brutal challenge than expected providing us with another island airfield to be used as a stepping stone to the Philippines.

After Biak, our search and destroy missions continued out of Hollandia up the coast of Dutch New Guinea without finding much to shoot at. We secured Vogelkop Peninsula. The Japanese were pulling back. We chased them. That was the program, chasing them or leaving them sweltering in a few isolated spots we bypassed. The U.S. and Australian victories in New Guinea were complete. The enemy here was soundly defeated. We had absolute supremacy in the air.

Late June 1944, now a full colonel, 26 years old, I was ordered back to Washington. After 24 months of pushing the bomb line 2,100 miles closer to victory, I came back to the States to present, as its commander, the Third Attack Group's objections to the A-26B we were testing for the final phase of the war.

It was difficult leaving this war, this terrible war not quite won. It was difficult leaving the command of the Third even though it would be in the capable hands of Lieutenant Colonel Richard Ellis, its Group Operations Officer and a pilot who came over from the States in 1942. Up and down the line, our best talent was in control with one thought: Get it over with.

It was difficult mustering up enthusiasm for the trip back to America. But thoughts of home and family and having a voice in the determination of the aircraft we would be using on our surge to victory eased the journey.

24

A-26B

PILOTS do speculate. Gather a group of pilots and soon they are concentrating on what could be . . . what might be . . . Redesigning their planes. Giving them more speed, better maneuverability, more guns, bigger payloads, better defenses. Warrior pilots have fantasies and opinions and recommendations that answer their needs in combat. Very often they are valid.

By the spring of 1944, many of the pilots flying out of New Guinea had been in combat with their B-25s and A-20s for more than two years. Their experience legitimatised the wealth of opinions and ideas they offered freely.

These were the men who had watched and worked out the evolution of the B-25 into the flying machine that made such a great contribution, relentlessly pushing the surviving "Sons of Heaven" out of their Southwest Pacific territory.

That early spring of 1944, hovering over the speculation were rumors of a new warplane being developed in California to replace the workhorses that had brought us as far as Nadzab, up the Markham Valley from Lae. Everyone in the field had heard descriptions of this new machine. No one then in our group had seen it. No official information was offered. No promises had been made and no schedules posted. Eventually we resigned ourselves to the status quo. We would, we surmised, be finishing the war with what we had.

Then, in May the rumors became more substantial. We learned that the new dream weapon would be arriving by ship at the new aircraft depot being developed at recently recaptured Finschhafen. What formerly had been a prime Japanese target would now be the site of assembly for the ultimate airplane. All indications were that this plane would take us to a new level of weaponry.

The plane's designation was A-26B, made by the Douglas Aircraft Company—the same company that developed and manufactured the A-20 that currently was serving us so well. The rumors promised it would be better than the A-20Gs we were flying.

And finally, toward the end of May, Bill Morrissey, the test pilot from the Douglas Long Beach, California plant, brought in the newly assembled A-26B from Finschhafen. Pilots, crews, staff, we were all impressed with the sight of that mighty bomber touching down on the Nadzab runway.

Being new almost was excitement enough to these war-weary combat crews of the Third.

This plane was more than new. It was a beauty. Its 41,000-plus pounds of gross weight, its 70-foot wing span were promises kept, The greatest piston engine ever built powered it. Each of its two 18-cylinder Pratt & Whitney R2800-27s put out 2,000 horsepower dry. Injecting water into the fuel to hype the engines further increased the power for short periods of time. It was a faster airplane than we were now flying.

The laminar flow wings were comparatively long and slim with double slotted flaps designed for lift, cruising speed and low landing speed. The bomb load at 6,000-pounds was more than double that of the A-20G and the range was more than 2,000 miles, twice and then some the A-20G's range. The A-26B as delivered to us was equipped with eight forward firing fifty-caliber Browning machine guns each with 500 rounds of ammo and two more in the upper rear power turret. A crew of three—pilot, navigator and rear gunner—would fly it.

In a few days, three more A-26Bs from Finschhafen followed for combat evaluation. Our Third Attack Group, longer in the theater with more combat experience than any other attack unit, would test it against the B-25s and A-20s we knew so well.

As Group Commander, I was first up. On June 7, 1944, Morrissey checked me out for local orientation and familiarization flights. Other pilots followed.

Then we headed out looking for suitable enemy targets that would provide live combat tests—short range search and destroy missions. None of them was worthy of the promise of our A-26B as a combat plane.

We flew further north. The nearest Japanese airfield and harbor of any consequence was Manokwari, another 375 miles northwest on the Vogelkop Peninsula. Our target was another disappointment. Making a minimum altitude pass we saw nothing but a few wrecked airplanes on the runways and a couple of damaged ships with a couple of tied up barges in the harbor. Not the formidable enemy we had sought.

We strafed and bombed anyway. We dropped our load of 20, 100-pound bombs along the north shore of the harbor encountering little ground fire—almost none. We had been briefed to expect no air opposition and, although ready, we got none.

The low-keyed missions did give us the opportunity to focus on the plane. Although we agreed the flying characteristics of the plane were excellent—good range, good bomb load, good engines—our overall reactions as low level bomber pilots were negative.

The cockpit arrangements were inefficient. Pilot visibility was hampered, making the minimum altitude formation flying so necessary to our bombing and strafing raids awkward. Both engines extended far forward of the pilot's position, at a level with his line of sight to the left, to the right and to the rear. It was like flying in a slit trench. Couldn't see down; couldn't see level. All you could see was up. That put pilots flying formation with a lead flying minimum altitude hanging on coconut trees or ship masts, or riding up his tail.

Inside a very wide cockpit, too wide for a single pilot airplane, was the seat and one control column placed on the left side, further disabling the pilot's right visibility,

The bomb bay doors were activated by a lever located forward to the right of the pilot seat forcing him to bend down and forward to reach it, again inhibiting his ability to see.

We flew the planes for a month. We tested them in combat singly and in formation against the enemy at Noemfoer, Biak Island, Wakde Island and Manokwari.

All the pilots who finished up the testing experienced similar difficulties. We concurred on the need to report negatively on our combat experiences with the new plane. It was a good single flight airplane, but not the plane for the tactics we were employing so successfully—low level strafing and bombing in tight formation primarily against Japanese shipping over scattered targets. We settled on 32 changes we would recommend be made in an effort to make the plane a combat formation plane usable by us in our kind of war.

We carried our list of 32 grievances with us when we consulted with the Fifth Bomber Command. It moved up with us when we discussed the airplane with the Fifth Air Force at Port Moresby. Our observations eventually reached the top, General, Kenney, and I was instructed to meet with him to give him our report first hand.

General George Kenney had been in the air attack business through 25 years of war, near war and peace. He understood our design problems immediately, placed me on temporary duty with orders to report to the Pentagon and deliver our list of A-26B design deficiencies. His goodbye was, "You go on home and tell them why we don't need it or want it! We'll stay with our B-25s, A-20s and B-24s."

The next day I was in Brisbane, Australia boarding a U.S. Navy flying boat heading east to Hawaii with priority travel orders taking me to Washington D.C. and Army Air Force Headquarters.

In spite of its faults, in the A-26B we were able to cruise at a speed of 235; our old B-25s cruised at 225 mph; the A-20s could push 234. Now, here I was trimmed back to the 120 mph top speed of this Navy flying boat, island hopping through the hot July heat from Australia to Pearl Harbor. It was a tedious trip. I survived for three days on sleeping potions provided by a flight surgeon in Brisbane who knew it would be a tedious trip. But I was 26 years old, confidently on my way to voice the criticisms made by my fellow experienced pilots who had taken the plane up and down the northern coast of New Guinea fighting the kind of intimate war this struggle for the Pacific had become.

From the Navy base at Pearl Harbor, I transferred to Hickam Field in Honolulu and boarded the newly-introduced Army Air Force Douglas C-54 that would transport me to Hamilton Field near San Francisco. The irony of the situation struck me as I sat within a Douglas product taking me toward Headquarters where I would lay out our 32 complaints we in the field had of another Douglas design.

Finally I was in the commercial comfort of an American Airlines DC-3, San Francisco to Washington D.C.—that is, San Francisco to Salt Lake City to Kansas City to Chicago to Washington D.C.

The finale of this journey back to America began with a phone number supplied me along with General Kenney's orders to return. It connected me to Brigadier General Bill Hipps, formerly of the Fifth Air Force at Port Moresby. I had befriended him there two years ago, well before he made general officer assigned to Headquarters.

Orders had me reporting at ten the next morning for the Pentagon meeting. Bill gave me the room number along with advice to come via the River entrance. That was the only information I had. At least I knew my contact, his phone number and where to start.

I was staying at the Statler, the first major hotel in Washington, D.C. constructed with integral air conditioning. What a wonder to this recent escapee from the equatorial heat. I plotted out the next day and stretched out on the cool white sheets pleased with my lot. When last I left the States I was a newly-appointed first lieutenant and my two years in the jungle had brought me back a war-wise colonel to an air conditioned room (no mosquito netting necessary here) and a meeting with experts at the Pentagon.

The following morning, well before 10 a.m., I was at the River entrance to the massive building as advised. The "good soldier" in me had me there early enough to guarantee my not missing the appointed time by even a minute.

The River entrance was the last landmark I was to find. At that entrance I showed my identification to the guard and asked directions to the room Bill had arranged. The security guard rattled off a series of turns and started me out. I originally took the series of rights and lefts I had remembered him instructing and ultimately ended up walking up and down stairs, stalking wide and narrow corridors (rings, insiders call them), in brightness and in dark and finally in despair, ending up in a great wide concourse overlooking an enclosed park. A splendid view but nowhere near where my A-26B audience was congregating or had already congregated since ten o'clock was now recent history.

We in the military had all heard the tale of the uniformed delivery boy who had lost his way in the Pentagon, emerging three years later an Admiral. I felt that I may be on a similar career path. President Dwight Eisenhower later gave the building grudging admiration when he proposed "it had apparently been designed to confuse any enemy which might infiltrate it." Robert McNamera called it "a jungle." My theory was an enemy could have contrived this building to bring the opposing leadership to ruin. I certainly felt beaten. All around me were people rushing in every way, apparently sure of their destinations. Some civilians. Others in uniforms of every stripe. All ranks. All services. All knowing where they were going.

Except me. I decided to swallow my pride. I was now a few minutes late for the meeting, wherever it was. I asked directions from the nearest person walking along with me. He was, shades of my past, an Army Air Force second lieutenant.

Was he acquainted with the building, I asked and sunk at his answer. "It all depends . . ."

I gave him the room number I had been seeking and he unblinkingly responded, "Yes, sir, that's in the Air Force section on the outer 4-E Ring. We are on the inner ring, four rings away." He was heading that way and offered to guide me there. That offer was a relief and I shamelessly admitted to him how much I appreciated the courtesy.

The meeting room was more than that. It was a grand conference room with an outer office presided over by a receptionist. The time was now ten minutes after ten when I introduced myself to her. She said yes, sir, I was expected and could go right in.

Inside I discovered "I was expected" by about a dozen-plus officers of higher rank than I had been anticipating, all arrived and seated. Three or four generals, several colonels, engineers, designers were waiting for me in their Pentagon attire. I was wearing my New Guinea khakis, shirt open. I was really flying solo on this mission.

Presiding was Lieutenant General Oliver Echols, a supply officer I had met before at our Group Headquarters at Dobodura. Our previous meeting coincided with the opening of "Tropical Paradise," a makeshift jungle officers club put together with palm leaves and bamboo and crowned with the "find" of the Third Attack Group—a blazing neon sign. His greeting was cordial and he introduced me to the other brass assembled, a few of whom I had met on the other side of the world. All waiting.

I tried to apologize for being late. General Echols tossed my apologies aside admitting that he suspected where the hell I had been. I confessed to being lost in the rings. That brought the house down. They were waiting for a cover-up explanation knowing that first-timers usually find themselves in the same predicament. The "Puzzle Palace" confuses them all and has been known to confound even some regular workers on duty there. My honesty warmed them.

Getting immediately to the business at hand, General Echols asked for my report on the A-26B. I started in on the list of findings in the field—all 32 of them, including the major items that posed serious complications for the crew plus some faults of lesser importance down to the location of the relief tubes.

General Echols politely allowed me to finish the report completely before he opened the group to discussion and questions.

I soon realized our findings from field tests and combat experience had preceded me to Washington via General Kenney. This group knew well our impression of the plane. This session was a serious follow-up probe to find out what had gone wrong with the design of this long-awaited weapon system. They were digging for answers beyond our 32 gripes that only field experience could give them. The session lasted through lunch, into the afternoon in an atmosphere of serious inquiry and investigation.

Their disappointment in the A-26B was no greater that ours. We wanted a new plane. We felt we needed a replacement for the 1930's designed B-25s and A-20s to take us through the war's final stages. We had no axe to grind regarding the design of this plane. But it did not measure up to our expectations. We called our shots as we lived them.

General Kenney had advised me when I left him in Brisbane, "Just tell them what you experienced. Be objective." I did that and I was that and I felt the respect they held for "a guy from the field" at the conclusion of my report.

Three days of meetings followed that first day-long session. I and my list of 32 faults must have visited every Army Air Force general's office. A few colonels' offices were thrown into my agenda. I learned my way around the rings of the Pentagon, not difficult once the "key" to the plan is found.

The reporting was finally finished. It had to be. There seemed to be no more generals in Washington to meet with me.

But yes, there was.

Instructions came down that I would report to "The Chief's" office. General of the Air Force. H. H. "Hap" Arnold. Himself. The man General Kenney said "lived with the throttle well open most of the time." What was I in for? Had I talked too much, too negatively, too imposingly in the previous meetings? What could he want with me?

Swiftly, before terror settled in, I was standing in Arnold's reception room with his aide instructing me to "go right in."

"Good morning, sir" was my best opening and I saluted, standing at very tight attention. He immediately put me "at ease" and cordially invited me to have a seat, querying me about Generals Kenney and Whitehead who were his World War I buddies in France.

And quickly his attention turned to the message I brought from the field. He questioned me extensively. Obviously his was first-hand knowledge of the A-26B and an intimate and discouraging awareness of our field findings. He admitted that he was very concerned and disappointed with our experiences with the plane and that he was looking for some way to overcome the A-26B's shortcomings.

Then, thank you and goodbye. End of interview. I was still breathing regularly with body intact and still in the Air Force, still wearing my eagles. And finally able to relax.

I had no right to be so content at that point. After the war ended I learned how deep was Arnold's disappointment. The plane had been his "baby" from conception to completion and he never totally accepted what went wrong. He had told Donald Douglas that he wanted that plane and that he should do what he had to do to get it sold. But he didn't murder the messenger, treating me courteously in a business-like fashion.

And, at the other end of the war and the other end of the spectrum was General Kenney sending me off unaware that his own opinion of the A-26B had long been negative. He felt the Allied efforts did not need the plane, that we were finally winning the Pacific war with adequately designed, combat tested equipment, the kind of equipment that was well-suited to Kenney's attack aviation tactics, that the A-26B was poorly designed and certainly not advanced enough for the post-war inventory he envisioned. Bulls had locked horns catching me between their eyeballs.

What carried me through those days in the Pentagon was my deep belief in our experience with planes and war—me and my fellow pilots—in our thorough and objective testing of the A-26B under combat conditions and in our need to express the disappointment we felt in this dream not delivered. We had no ulterior motives. We were not playing product politics.

I stayed Stateside three months going from the Pentagon to the Douglas aircraft factory to Wright Field Engineering Center to Eglin Field Proving Ground Command. I revisited my old Notre Dame campus. I married Mary McGuire and honeymooned. Ultimately I reported to Hamilton Field near San Francisco to arrange transportation back to New Guinea to rejoin the Third, still encamped in the hills of Hollandia. Waiting for space, my new bride and I camped out in the great historic St. Francis Hotel atop Nob Hill for $12.00 a night. The hotel currently describes itself as "the destination and meeting place for many famous guests throughout its history . . . to bask in the elegant comfort of the hotel." Bask we did.

General MacArthur also used the hotel as his headquarters later when he returned to the United States in 1951. His was a suite, now named after him. Unfortunately the wait was brief and I was cleared to board a C-54 to return on October 20, 1944.

The news that day was MacArthur's return to the Philippines—his promise fulfilled. U.S. forces had landed on an island called Leyte, wherever the hell that was. I would soon learn.

We had thought the landing would be on the southern-most island of the Philippines, Mindanao. Fooled us. Fooled the Japanese. Skipped a few miles north and landed on Leyte. The "Old Man" had been leapfrogging up the Pacific for months and he did it again.

Mary McGuire and John Henebry at their wedding reception

My flight left from Hamilton for Hickam at Pearl Harbor then island hopped to Nadzab where I snatched a B-25 to put me back in the saddle of the Third at Hollandia. Just in time to get ready for our move to Leyte and beyond.

Leyte

IF Leyte were to be the new battleground, it was out of range for our A-20s based at Sentani outside of Hollandia. The A-20s of the Third were designated to be the first to re-enter the Philippines on bombing missions. Two thousand miles going northwest lay between the sites. Not an airfield between except at Owi, an island 270 miles off the southeast coast in the Biak complex. The next touchdown was Tacloban on Leyte. Again we needed to pack and go to keep in this war.

The word came only a few days after I returned to Hollandia that Leyte, now captured and secured, soon would be stabilized enough to move our A-20s into an air-ground support position. The great Naval battle of Leyte Gulf on the east had just been won driving what remained of the Japanese naval forces out of the area. Our ground forces had cleared the Japanese off the west coast of the island but were having trouble forcing them out of Ormoc Bay, on the northwest point of Leyte. Aside from this remaining Japanese ground resistance, Leyte was ours—secure but a little unsettled.

Establishing our fighter aircraft and bombers at Tacloban would mark the greatest advance of the bomb line in the war to date. It was, incidentally, MacArthur's first station after graduation from West Point. Our presence at Tacloban was essential to recapturing the whole of the Philippines. And then moving on to Japan.

Headquarters dispatched me to determine what airfields would be coming available to us. In a B-25D with enough range to reach Tacloban via Owi I flew out of Hollandia into the only available field on Leyte, it with limited operations. Army construction engineers had not been able to unload enough men and equipment to fix up airfields, let alone roads.

Primary traffic on Tacloban for the past week had been Navy aircraft which had been forced to use the island airstrip as an alternate landing site during

Admiral Halsey's classic engagement with the Japanese Navy concurrent with the Leyte landing and occupation.

The facility had become overcrowded. Damaged and crash-landed planes were bulldozed into the sea to make room for subsequent take-offs and landings, a lesson taken from aircraft carrier operations during battle.

Runway and parking space for Air Force planes was so limited at Tacloban that General Kenney himself had personally taken over the supervision of the needed construction work. Lieutenant Colonel Pappy Gunn, with 1,500 Filipinos recruited to speed the work, was contributing his ingenious efforts to creating operational airfields. That inspiration ended when a lone Japanese plane penetrated our defenses, dropping an incendiary bomb on the airdrome construction. A phosphorous fragment lodged in Pappy's left arm. Wounded, he was taken from his Jeep on the runway area and evacuated to Brisbane.

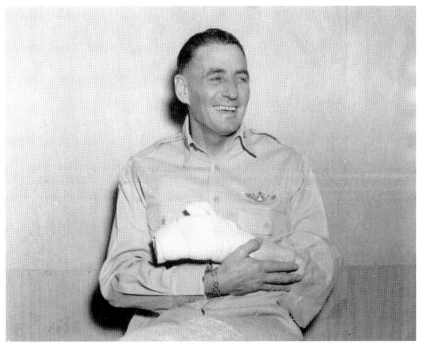

"Pappy" Gunn (1945) recovering from his wound inflicted by a strafing Japanese plane

Contributing to the confusion was the instability of the earth and the heavier than normal rainfall. Northeastern Leyte was rice paddy country. Our heavy construction and transportation equipment chewed up what few roads we had inherited. Within a few days of Allied arrival the roads had disappeared into the soggy ground.

On my arrival there were no airstrips available for our Hollandia-based A-20s. What airfields the engineers were planning to rig up would be for the exclusive use of P-38 fighter aircraft.

179

Their priority status rested in the bitter success of a new Japanese offensive strategy inaugurated October 25, 1944—Admiral Takijiro Onishi's swarming Kamikaze attacks. Desperate young Japanese pilots diving their bomb-laden aircraft into Allied ships in suicidal attacks could be stopped only by our intercepting fighters or our ground- or ship-based anti-aircraft guns filling the air with flak. Twenty seconds from the time the plane came into view was the total time available to destroy the aircraft. Those planes, not stopped, annihilated aircraft carriers, cruisers and destroyers, sinking more ships than traditional weapons had been able to destroy. The combat brought the American sailors manning the guns to the breaking point. Battle fatigue increased alarmingly.

At the time of the Leyte invasion, the numbers of suicide planes and pilots this radical enemy had available to throw against the Allies were astounding. By war's end thousands of enemy pilots had sacrificed themselves, ultimately including Onishi himself whose suicide note asked atonement for "the souls of you who fell gallantly as human bullets." The nightmare of the Philippines climaxed with 36 ships sunk, more than 350 damaged, almost 5,000 wounded men and 5,000 dead.

With no airfield space available and those coming available delegated to P-38s I was told to return to the Third Attack Group at Hollandia. I did.

Late in November 1944, while we and our planes still sat impatiently in Hollandia, engineers completed an airstrip in the Halmahera Islands, half-way between Biak and Leyte. At the same time the Leyte-based engineers were making progress on their runway construction. These reports were enough to give us a January date for moving our ground echelon and equipment to what was becoming our Philippine stronghold.

The Third came to Leyte by convoy, an uneventful south sea island cruise from Hollandia to a beach just south of the town of Dulag. It left behind its planes and pilots waiting for the completion of a runway to welcome us. Flying back into Tacloban, I joined all four squadrons and Group Headquarters at our designated location on the Leyte Gulf beach in an idyllic tree grove, a former coconut plantation.

The LSTs (Landing Ship-Tank) were beached and our first order of business was to off-load our equipment and personnel, since the LSTs were vulnerable to the continuing Kamikaze attacks.

Leyte Gulf was filled with U.S. Navy combat ships and loaded transport ships, great targets not unnoticed by the Japanese, smarting from their defeats and counter-offensing with their Kamikaze suicides. The day before our LST arrival a Kamikaze had hit the USS *Nashville* directly on the bridge, killing many of the crew, including Air Force Colonel Jack Mertha who was on board liaising with other Army and Navy officers.

But until we had our planes we could only watch the grim tactics of war from our temporary home on the beach facing east overlooking Leyte Gulf—

the desperate death dives, the fireworks displays created by our shore- and ship-based antiaircraft defenders, P-38s shooting down enemy aircraft.

The P-38s had great cheering sections on the relatively under-armed transport ships bringing in the backup stuff of battle. They waited to be unloaded like sitting ducks. The P38s were their protective angels.

We watched them arrive from the States; we watched them wait; we watched them unload their cargo of bombs, ammunition, bombsights, carefully packed and protected by unlimited amounts of 4×12-inch planks; we watched them throw the now useless lumber overboard.

The lumber was not deemed useless by one Lieutenant Phillips, an imaginative, intelligent, ambitious and opportunistic operator. "Those planks," he mused, "just what we need for tent floors at our new camp."

Phillips, tall, blond, slim, on-the-move, began moving in on the lumber. He started with a couple bottles of whiskey of unknown source bringing them to an Army Engineering company operating the amphibious trucks used to unload the bombs from the ships. The whiskey sealed the deal allowing him use of the trucks.

As whiskey was a latchkey to the engineers, the transport ships' captains and crews bowed to P-38 pilots who shot down Kamikazes. Phillips was not a pilot but he knew what they looked like. With his borrowed pilot's wings and his assumed pilot swagger and his commandeered amphibious truck he moved on to the Gulf, calling on the ships captains. He sold his story that he was a pilot in a P-38 squadron in need of all the lumber he could put his hands on. Would they save it for him rather than throw it overboard? of course they would for this protector. They would hold it; he would pick it up.

And so it came to pass that every tent in the Third's coconut grove had a timber floor. Beats sand when you are trying to put your socks on. Keeps your feet dry during the notable Philippine rains.

We continued sitting planeless but substantially housed on our tropical island beach amidst the coconut trees. Life was dull for us. Then the monsoons hit. A tent camp on a beach is not the fortification needed. Half our tents were knocked down, mine included. The horizontal rains coming in the middle of the tropical night are cold and wet. And destructive. No one was hurt but it took a better part of a week to put our camp back together again. Then life returned to dull.

Another water problem surfaced, to my surprise. Our supply and mess officers informed me that the Third did not have any drinking water. It was a detail that had not been a concern since our medical officer had confirmed that our source of water, a nearby well-head that U.S. Engineers had drilled, was putting out an abundance of clean, sweet water.

The driver of our tank truck had gone over to fill up one morning and was met by an armed guard from the Seventh Infantry Division, our good neighbors. The guard denied him access to the well.

The driver commented that there appeared to be plenty of water. "That doesn't make any difference," retorted the guard, "I have been ordered not to let anyone but soldiers from this division have any."

The Third driver tried to reason that the water was going to friendly troops, that we were all fighting the same enemy. This rationale didn't make any difference. If we wanted water from that well we would need permission from his division headquarters.

Our Group supply officer followed up and heard the same line. He went to the infantry division engineering officer who told him "no dice," these were orders from the division commander, a Major General John Hodge. Attempting to go up the command ladder, the adjutant told our supply officer that General Hodge would see only his commanding officer—me—if I so desired to pursue the matter.

You bet I did. We needed the water, we had as much right to it as the infantry and I took a Jeep and drove over to the division headquarters where the adjutant immediately showed me into the General's tent.

Saluting, I quickly introduced myself with no small talk preliminaries. Hodge returned my salute and without the courtesy of putting me at ease he announced that we were not to use "his" well because he had commandeered it for the exclusive use of his soldiers.

At the conclusion of this announcement a plane flew low over his headquarters tent. He, his adjutant and another officer in attendance jumped from their camp chairs and dove under their desks. I remained at attention, recognizing from the sound that the plane was unmistakably a B-25, a sound I would not readily forget.

I stood alone at attention in the middle of the tent while the low-flying B-25 quickly passed. When the sound subsided my hosts sheepishly reappeared from under their desks with silly looks on their faces.

The General said, "What the hell was that?"

"A B-25, sir," said I feeling some little compassion for the extent of combat these three must have been through.

But the General continued his harangue about the well. I saluted and excused myself and he shouted after me, "If you want to cry to Papa, go right ahead. The water is ours." "Papa" to him was General Whitehead.

If "Papa's" intervention was what he prescribed it was to "Papa" I would go. My men needed the water that Yank engineers had provided. I had no other choice. Whitehead sent Major General "Fighter" Hutchinson back with me to iron out the problem. What a useless exercise, convincing the Infantry that the Air Force was an integral part of the Allied effort.

When our planes finally arrived, we were eager and ready to join in the move toward victory. Enough of box seats at the battle, manipulating supply lines, monsoons and skirmishes with the infantry. It was still a long way to Tokyo.

Back to New Guinea

THE war was moving forward in giant leaps according to MacArthur's agenda and had been sweeping me along with it.

By the end of January 1945 our group had moved north from Leyte on the east of the Philippines to Mindoro on its west. The Japanese were losing the Philippines and knew they had lost the war. But this was an enemy who would not surrender. Surrender brought disgrace to the warrior, to family and to country. He fought hard and died hard. His code offered no other options.

I was settling in when a call came from General Kenney asking me to meet him back at Tacloban air strip just above Leyte the following morning. Flying over early, I was waiting at the flight line when Kenney's Jeep brought him from town where he and General MacArthur were maintaining their Philippine headquarters.

Not prone to casual visits, Kenny's invitation was a command performance and I had been curious and apprehensive about the call. He emerged from the Jeep and jumped into the meat of the matter. He was moving Colonel Carl Brandt into command of the Thirteenth Air Force, reestablishing a base in the Halmahera Islands, above Indonesia halfway to the Philippines. Kenney wanted me to follow Brandt as head of the Combat Readiness Training Center (CRTC) at Nadzab.

Back to New Guinea for me. Back to the beautiful Markham River Valley. Out of the fight. This most drastic career change of my life was taking me out of active combat command. My days on the bomb line were over. They had been strenuous and bold and had catapulted me up the ranks from a first lieutenant to an eagle colonel. Their ferociousness had put a Purple Heart, an Air Medal with its Oak Leaf cluster, a Distinguished Flying Cross with three Oak Leaf clusters, a Silver Star and a Distinguished Service Cross on my chest. I had flown over 200 combat missions.

Colonel Carl Brandt and John Henebry at CRTC

Kenney felt now the CRTC assignment would be an interesting interim challenge. It proved to be.

The CRTC was begun a couple of years into the war as an orientation program for all air crew members coming from the States assigned to the flying units of the Far East Air Force. A first stop was Nadzab and "Post graduate" instruction to bring them up to speed in gunnery, bombing, air-to-air fighter tactics, jungle survival, aircraft identification, ship recognition, communications and tropical mountain flying.

Orientation was very real. Although New Guinea was ours—we had bypassed several hot spots from Rabaul, to the Admiralty Islands to Wewak, generally quieting the terrain—every now and then our air crews would experience some anti-aircraft fire from Japanese hold-outs on the ground. They did some damage to aircraft but we never lost a plane nor a crew member and secretly we were grateful to the Japanese for their relatively risk-free contribution to this phase of "graduate" combat training before the aviators joined their operational units in the Philippines and Okinawa.

The activity of our trainees on the other hand kept the Japanese alert and aware that we were still serious about waging war and that their enemies were winning it.

We now owned the sky and the land under it. At Nadzab we had room to spare to improve our air operations, so we had constructed gunnery, strafing and low level bombing ranges.

Colonel John Alison and Colonel Phil Cochran, who both led the U.S. air effort in the China-Burma-India Theater and flew with General Chennault's Flying Tigers against the Japanese, discussed tactical issues with the CRTC, during a stop in New Guinea, about the move on to the Philippines. In the final year of the war, Alison became operations officer of the Fifth Air Force, which continued its movement through the Southwest Pacific and finally on to Japan.

At this point in World War II, Germany and Italy having surrendered, we began receiving even more airplanes, equipment and personnel than had previously been assigned to the Far East Theater. The base was equipped with a flight of every type of plane in use in the theater—B-24s, B-25s, A-20s, P-38s, P-40s, P-51 Mustangs and a flight of P-47s—all at my disposal as commander of the base. I was checked out in and did fly every one of them, making a conscientious effort to become familiar with each.

One of the great pleasures for John Henebry, and a wonderful sense of comfort for their mother, was being able to meet up with his brother Joe during one of his stops at Nadzab.

A favorite was the P-38. I later flew several missions over the hills of Luzon against pockets of Japanese hold-outs. The plane was a twin engine fighter with two quiet liquid cooled in-line engines with counter rotating props. The propellers going in the opposite direction eliminated the torque, particularly at full power takeoff. Later, when I flew jets, I realized it was the same sensation as the counter-rotating props of the P-38. A powerful pleasure to fly.

In addition to combat training, we became a holding center for new crews. As the fighting units rotated their crew members home after completing their combat tours, they would requisition from CRTC the numbers of pilots, gunners and navigators that would bring their units up to strength. Personnel at the base were now numbering eight to ten thousand. This now being the only war in town, a stream of VIPs from the Pentagon, from the media, others intent on touring the theater continually swelled the ranks.

We had become an impressive population and whenever I contacted headquarters I reminded those powers of our numbers and urged them to route USO entertainers around our way.

So we saw and appreciated talent coming and going. One of the most impressive shows was "Mexican Hayride," directed and produced by Irving Berlin who accompanied his troupe through the Far East. Berlin staged three or four performances at Nadzab to audiences of thousands, everyone enthusiastic about the talent.

Irving Berlin with John Henebry

I had constructed a rather hospitable shack sitting all by itself high on the hills of Nadzab and Berlin stayed with me during the two or three weeks he "Played" the Pacific. His vocal renditions of his songs filled the night air during the impromptu after-hours piano sessions that became a regular diversion.

His one request was to tour Mt. Hagen, in the highlands 5,000 feet above sea level, some 50 miles northwest of Nadzab. The altitude produced very comfortable tropical temperatures and a concentrated display of unusually beautiful flowers and the classic birds-of-paradise. According to a couple of Catholic missionaries who had lived in a Mt. Hagen residence for several years, the place had been brought to the attention of the world only as recently as 1930 when Michael Leahy, an Australian prospector, came upon it and its stone-age people in search of gold.

Uneventfully I flew Berlin up to Mt. Hagen in our twin engine executive Beechcraft C-45. The excitement began as I attempted an ultimately successful landing on a narrow strip of mowed grass about 2,000 feet long serving as the Mt. Hagen runway. A tight fit even for this utility airplane we used for private transportation. While I struggled with the dimensions, Berlin was captivated by the attitude of the nationals who looked upon the "balus"—the big metal bird—with great amazement and curiosity. White men and their airplanes were still astonishing sights to a village that a dozen years before thought the entire world was contained on this mountain top.

Irving Berlin with John Henebry at Mt. Hagen with some of the local villagers

Another celebrity surfaced at Nadzab during my tenure. In the spring of 1945 my father-in-law in Chicago sent along the news that Dr. Charles Mayo was serving in the Army, someplace in New Guinea. The couple of doctors attached to CRTC knew of no Dr. Mayo so I called the Army Station Hospital asking the operator if he knew of a Dr. Mayo from the Midwest serving in the area.

"I sure do," the operator responded. "The hospital commander here is Colonel Mayo. Is he the one? Let's put him on the line and we can find out."

And he sure was. Dr. Charles Mayo was heading a whole unit brought over from his renowned Mayo Clinic in Minnesota. It unofficially bore his name—The Mayo Unit.

Dr. Charles Mayo and John Henebry at Nadzab in 1945

My favorite medical man, Doc Gilmore, would come through Nadzab after he was assigned to the 308th Bomb Wing. During one visit the commander of the Australian troops based in Lae called to invite us down for dinner. I accepted but warned Doc, "when they start their 'Hail to the Queen' stuff with that Australian rot gut, we are out of there!"

We took my Beechcraft the 18 miles down the Markham Valley to the dinner party. As dark descended and the Australians began their expected hailing the Queen, we did join them, at first out of courtesy and later for the sport of it.

The next morning, when I realized I was in my own bed, I yelled out to Doc, "Where's the airplane?"

"Jeez, Jock, I don't have the least idea," came the muffled answer from the next room.

So we jumped into the Jeep parked in front of my shack and hightailed it down to the airstrip where we found the Beechcraft parked perfectly. Through war and mischievousness, I remained the pilot.

CRTC headquarters moved to Clark Field, north of Manila, the old regular Army Air Corps base in the Philippines that was the second strike, after Pearl Harbor, the Japanese made against the U.S. four years previous. The environs of Clark provided our flight crews with a little scrapping from some Japanese hold-outs in the hills of Luzon.

We continued to coordinate with all of the Allied Forces in the final push to

Japan. I was called to Okinawa to plan for the Allied invasion of Japan and the final surrender by Japan. The atomic bomb attacks on August 6 and 9, 1945, precluded the necessity of an invasion, and Japan soon surrendered.

On August 14, 1945, General Kenney suspended all further combat missions in the Pacific Theater. Two weeks later Dick Ellis, Chuck Howe and I flew a symbolic attack formation into Japan and landed at Atsugi Field with the first of the Third Attack Group planes. The Third Attack Group moved to Atsugi and remained based in Japan for several years.

Mac and Me

HE preceded me to Australia by three months, but I was there to watch him leave the Pacific.

We were to fight a couple of grizzly wars together.

He was a stately man when I first served under him, and elegant still nine years later at his goodbye.

Now there he was that first time in my line of vision, poised to exit the AMP Insurance Building elevator as the doors slid open and here I was, paralyzed with wonder, blocking his way.

The nine-story AMP Insurance Building in downtown Brisbane, Australia was a typical modern high rise office building. During the period when the Japanese were threatening invasion of the mainland, businesses moved south to Sydney, AMP being one of them. Our Fifth Air Force operations had moved into its evacuated city structure and I was there on bomber business on this refreshingly cool winter day.

The AMP Building also housed the command headquarters for the Allied Forces in the Soutwest Pacific Area.

Tracking the elevator on the overhead indicator as it descended toward the lobby, I had positioned myself directly in front of the doors, eager to get in and on with the purpose of my business in town. As operations officer of the Ninetieth Squadron, I was reviewing our Group's and the Fifth Bomber Command's response to the characteristics of our newly converted B-25Cs.

Even my appearance before the headquarters staff was secondary to my initial assignment of picking up another of the 16 converted bombers from Eagle Farms.

Just in from the bush, in leather flight jacket and flight cap, even though I was a captain, I must have looked like the shaggy combat pilot I was at heart.

He, on the other hand, looked like the four-star general he was—resplendent. The elevator doors opened and we stood face to face. My mind, training and instincts ordered me to step back and salute our redeemer, our creator of the heavens and war-torn earth as we now knew it, allowing this Supreme Commander, with his single military escort, to pass. But my body remained immobile, my mouth agape for a instant of paralyzed awe.

In a second instant I did step back, salute and surprise myself by enunciating a crisp "Good morning, sir" instead of "aga aba oog."

General Douglas MacArthur returned my salute, said "good morning, captain" and was out on the street before I could blink again. The door closed and the elevator rose without me while I stood entranced, watching him smartly leave the building and disappear into his waiting staff car.

He was in uniform, of course, cutting quite a figure. It was July 1943, winter in Australia and "down under" cool, and the General wore a handsomely tailored tunic with his four stars defining his strong shoulders, his ribbons climbing up to his left epaulet. The whole impressive outfit was topped off with that unorthodox battered and braided cap that years before had became a symbol of his power as Marshall of the Philippine military forces.

As he marched out the door, the power of his presence remained. His handsomeness. His uniform, the most elaborate I had seen in this war. The stars glowing on his shoulders. The riot of color of his service ribbons. Used as I was to the vigor of the young men with whom I associated, his 62-year-old face had surprising power and freshness. His walk was brisk. His body was trim. He was in great physical shape in spite of his recent war experiences and escape from Bataan. He was an old man nobly holding his own in a young man's army.

But he was not as tall as I would have expected, being the nature of heroes to grow tall in our imaginations.

A couple of days later the current B-25 conversion was complete and I took it back to Seventeen-Mile, my hot jungle base outside of Port Moresby, where our Squadron Commander Major Ed Larner snarled, "Where the hell have you been?" Too many days away from the war zone must have put a look of contentment on my face.

I reviewed my trip to Brisbane to bring back a converted B-25, shared some boulevard commando tales and finished off with a brief reference to a meeting with General MacArthur.

"The hell, you say," said Larner, "what'd he have to do with you?"

I assured him that it was a very cordial meeting, that we came to a perfectly agreeable conclusion, but ultimately had to confess that I had said a mere "Good morning, Sir," and he had concurred with "Good morning."

Larner felt confident that no smart-ass behavior had obstructed the war effort nor blighted the reputation of our squadron or the Air Force.

Face-to-face contact with MacArthur was a rarity for most of the men who served under him in the Pacific war. We hardly ever saw him from a distance, much less up close.

Nor did we hear much from him or of him aside from a few announcements or communiques. Our major sources of MacArthur news came from Tokyo Rose, *The Stars and Stripes*, an infrequent Australian newspaper or radio broadcast or a stray magazine.

He was austere and ungregarious. He never visited our unit and I don't know of any that he did. He ran his air war from reports of how and what we were doing, submitted by Generals Kenney and Whitehead, whose information came from their staffs and subordinate commanders—group commanders, fighters, bombers, transport and depot operators. He was always aware of combat results through Kenney's frequent and detailed operational reports.

Later in the war, when I moved up to Group Headquarters and traveled in a nearer orbit, infrequently we would be in contact with General Kenney or some of his staff and some MacArthur anecdotes would be passed along to us. Now and then someone heard of someone glimpsing him as he passed through an airport, coming or going here or there.

Our boss, Kenney, as MacArthur's head airman, was one of the few with intimate and easy access to the General. As the success of the air war mounted, MacArthur's confidence in Kenney's ability to establish and maintain dependable air power nurtured a solid personal relationship between the two men.

This aloofness toward others was not forced. He was not trying to create mystery. He was extremely busy and his time was carefully used. And, this being a military structure, the man at its pinnacle was treated with total formality.

Later, after the ground troops had moved through New Guinea and the Halmaheras and had secured Leyte in the Philippines, the area had quieted down. Our group of four squadrons was camped in the coconut grove waiting to be moved to Mindoro, one of the Philippines' central islands.

To liven up this quiet came a message from General Ennis C. Whitehead, the commander of the Fifth Air Force advance echelon, inviting me to a ceremony at Tacloban Airfield.

Congress had awarded Major Richard I. Bong its Medal of Honor. Dick had recently shot down his fortieth Japanese plane, making him the leading United States war ace covering all theaters of war. He superceded Eddie Rickenbacker with his World War I record of 22 planes and four balloons.

This ceremony would be a rare and treasured occasion in which those of us in combat could witness a buddy being honored as a living, breathing hero, a survivor of battles in a war that was taking its toll.

Bong was in the Forty-Ninth Group based near my camp at Leyte. I flew a couple of P-38 fighter missions with the Forty-Ninth and was part of his cheering squad as he racked up his kills. Dick was as easy-going a guy as he was a fantastic pilot and enjoyed his competition with his fellow Forty-Ninth Group

Major Dick Bong received the Congressional Medal of Honor from
General Douglas MacArthur in the Philippines as the leading United States War Ace.

pilot Tommy McGuire as top war ace. Tommy later was knocked down over
Clark Field with 38 victories.

The Theater Commander himself, General Douglas MacArthur, would be
presenting the medal and he would note with satisfaction that Dick would receive
it alive and well.

I certainly would be there.

The General was his majestic, theatrical self. He was a masterful center of
ceremony. But since his unfulfilled promise to return to Manila was still ringing
in the Pacific air the ceremony was simple. MacArthur made it impressive.

Gathered at Tacloban air strip for Bong's honors were the General's staff,
General George Kenney and as many Army Air Force brass as could be spared
away from the duties of war. Amid all this luster, MacArthur remained the focus.

He instinctively played all the moves to add grandeur to this day. Before and
after the ceremony he was graciously congenial. During the ceremony, he was
brief and electric.

He and we enjoyed every facet of the presentation.

I didn't personally see the General again until August 1945 when the Japanese
realized they had had enough and finally decided to hang it up. Then, the brass of
the Advanced Occupation Forces met on Okinawa to discuss MacArthur's

entrance to Japan and the imminent formal surrender ceremonies. General Kenney was part of this planning group and had me, as 360th Wing Commander, join in the meeting.

While I was conferring with Kenney, General MacArthur arrived with full entourage. MacArthur, now with five stars and a General of the Armies title, and his high ranking star-studded staff quickly established priority over—and ended—my conference with Kenney.

He first expressed personal greetings to the rank on hand and shook hands all around. It was an informal, unheralded appearance of a well-known figure and the men on the field began to notice, yet keeping their distance. In spite of the impromptu casualness of the gathering, military decorum prevailed, as it will to a high degree when brass rubs against brass, particularly at this level of polish.

I stepped aside, deferring to the obvious business at hand of arranging MacArthur's movement to a designated meeting place on the base.

Having backed off, I was able to watch the General as he stood aloof on the fringes of the gathered personnel intent on settling the details of this urgent and unscheduled meeting.

No one stood very close to the General. Remote, he was patiently waiting for his administrators to agree upon the next move. As the arrangements began to gel during this stand-up confab, now and then General Kenney or the General's Chief of Staff, Lieutenant General Sutherland, would step over to have a word with him—questioning a detail or seeking concurrence with a suggestion.

During the entire time the General surveyed the growing crowd. He slowly turned through every point of the compass as though he were studying the couple dozen or so soldiers, airman, marines and sailors on the periphery and the landscape beyond them. In doing so he allowed the spectators to see him. His egocentricity assured him all were looking. He gave everyone the opportunity for a camera shot of that legendary profile crowned by that famous crazy cap. Only the corncob pipe was missing.

Even though the crowd expectedly was subdued I had the feeling that these few representative warriors, who had been through such a long, treacherous battle, were jubilantly appreciating this close up view at last of the great leader with his own exemplary war record who had brought them to this victory.

When the immediate plans were finalized, the General moved to the arriving cars. It was dignified movement. His demeanor generated an aura of respect and as the cars carefully drove away no rousing hoopla sent them off, only a courteous round of applause. The lord of the war had arrived, appeared to us all and moved on.

As the business of ending the war moved on, I was reassigned to Atsugi, a Japanese air base near Tokyo Bay, some 15 miles west of Yokohama. General MacArthur arrived there the same day as I, August 28, 1945, to accept Japan's formal surrender five days hence.

September 2nd, Tokyo Bay was the backdrop, filled with 216 warships anchored in majestic array. Vast as the stage was, the focus of attention remained 18 miles offshore on the showman MacArthur aboard the USS *Missouri*, the 45,000 ton "Mighty Mo," selected in honor of President Harry S. Truman's home state.

Although flanked by scores of general and flag officers representing the United States and all the victorious allies, facing a diplomatic and military contingent representing the vanquished enemy—its navy in white, its army without sword in khaki, its diplomats without flag in cutaways and tall hats—although standing aboard the quarter deck of this majestic, outmoded man-o'-war offering an array of gun turrets and cable and steel, MacArthur remained the catalytic character of the unfolding drama.

Surrounding the main arena over an area the size of three football fields were crowded the working press from countries around the globe and witnesses outside the official party, including me. Thousands of us were crammed onto the massive ship, on the mast and smokestacks, gripping railings, draping over turrets and ten- and sixteen-inch gun barrels, swarming over the awesome teak decks, eyes centered on the table draped in green, on the documents of surrender, ecstatic to be part of this concluding act of war.

As grand drama, never was there created a more impressive scene, impeccably detailed down to the fountain pens used to sign the papers. It was a fitting ceremony. It was powerful and moving. It was joyous to those of us who had struggled to arrive at this place.

The actual unconditional proceedings were very solemn—formal and militarily proper. MacArthur rose to a grandeur that befitted the occasion. He played and was the legitimate heroic figure in this now-ended tragedy.

His message to the vanquished was short, firm, direct, positive and polite, encompassing both military and diplomatic courtesies. His final words were succinct, powerfully delivered, ringing out: These proceedings are closed. Then the sun shone from behind clouds and 2,000 airplanes swept over the bay.

His words spoke the thoughts of the many warriors here in awesome attendance in the company of their recent enemy. They soothed the emotions over lost friends who came out of this battle with only posthumous awards. Suddenly amidst the grandeur of this day, September 2, 1945, the months and years that preceded seemed so useless. Ten million lives spent in this Pacific war. Those three years I had labored in this theater with all the others sacrificing young men's time and young men's lives.

What was the withered and frail Lieutenant General Wainwright thinking, standing there with MacArthur, having arrived in Yokohama only a couple of days earlier following his release from a Japanese prisoner of war camp in China? After marching to Pampanga. After being shipped in a boxcar from Luzon to Panay. After a diet of rice, potatoes, mango beans and coconut lard. After three years of filth and maggots. "Bring skinny over" was an instinctive

The deck of the USS *Missouri* on September 2, 1945, for the formal surrender ceremony

detail of this MacArthur-designed day and Jonathan Wainwright watched up close in silence.

When the hard fought war was over, the struggle for peace replaced it. President Truman, acting under the dictates of the agreement at Potsdam, named MacArthur the Supreme Commander, Allied Powers (SCAP). His job: rebuild Japan.

He was the designated peacemaker but as U.S. Commander in the Far East he eventually found himself stemming another war in a neighboring land, Korea. As the Communists in the north rushed to claim the land of South Korea, MacArthur was named commander of the United Nations to formalize the attempt to halt the land grab.

The initial defeat of the North Koreans brought in Communist China, sending troops to rescue North Korea in its now-floundering effort to save the government and the northern territory. The presence of the Chinese complicated MacArthur's agenda.

The U.N. leadership balked at the potential scope of this newly expanded war. Policy decisions were made counter to MacArthur's judgement on the course of the war. MacArthur, who had had such a profound influence on the course of military history, was meeting major opposition in Washington and New York. While disagreement between warriors and politicians is not criminal, airing it publicly, using the press as a platform borders on a serious infraction of expected behavior.

The initial, the basic, the primary lesson the military teaches is: DO NOT TRY TO BUCK THE SYSTEM. Privates learn it quickly. Generals have long ago learned it and rarely forget it. I learned it the day I joined the Army Air Corps, even before I was issued my orders. I learned it innocently but I learned it well from the first officer I encountered as a recruit.

Notre Dame scheduled my class of '40 graduation ceremonies at South Bend for the same day that the Army ordered me to report for my swearing in at the Federal Building in Chicago.

When I received notice that my application to enter Army Air Corps flight training had been accepted with the orders to report, I realized my dilemma. I headed for the Notre Dame registrar to enlist his help. I explained my desire to both graduate with my class in person and report as a Flying Cadet. I expressed my fear that if I didn't join the Army on its appointed day I would be set back a whole pilot training class. Fate had assigned me to 41B, the second class to be graduated in the year 1941, and I wanted to follow its dictates.

The registrar was sympathetic and, not having a military mind-set, promised to look into the situation. Two days later his good news was that Army brass at Fort Sheridan had given permission for me to report a day late yet remain in my originally assigned 41B.

A perfect solution. My family could come to my graduation and drive me back to Chicago and my 9 a.m. appointment in the Federal Building on Jackson Boulevard, Chicago.

And at 9 a.m. there I was, fresh from the strains of "Pomp and Circumstance," stating my business to a front desk Army clerk who directed me to the office of the commander of the detachment, a major, spic and span, trim down to his riding britches and highly polished boots. In downtown Chicago? Where did he park his horse, I wondered. Was I joining the Calvary or the Air Corps? I was a cocky recruit.

In response to my name and the nature of my business he said, "Oh, yes. Henebry. We got word from Fifth Army Headquarters at Fort Sheridan that you would be reporting a day late. Now go out to the adjutant, have him swear you into the service, get your travel orders and then come back here. I want to talk to you." A little less cocky, I wondered what the hell he wanted to see me about.

But I went to the adjutant, a captain, and with the raising of my right hand I was in the Army and waiting for my orders making me Flying Cadet John P. Henebry A0406548 and my travel orders assigning me to Spartan School of Aeronautics in Tulsa Oklahoma for Primary Pilot Training.

My first order as a Cadet was to report back to the breeched and booted major.

"Henebry," he bellowed, "you are now in the Army. Congratulations. But I want to give you some advice. We gave you a date to report and you wanted a new one. So you and Notre Dame went over our heads directly to Fifth Army Headquarters at Fort Sheridan. You will learn real soon that you should never go out of regular channels over your superiors' heads. We have a system in the Army and YOU WILL NOT BUCK THE SYSTEM." The final statement was carefully enunciated.

The finality of his statement implied that this was no time to ask questions or offer explanations. Lesson learned, I responded, "Yes, sir," departed for the station and the train to take me to Tulsa, Spartan School, primary flying classes and, wise to the ways of the military, the beginning of a long cooperative adventure with the Army Air Corps and its subsequent USAAF and USAF.

The confrontation with the major ended with that day. I never heard again of my "out of channel" swearing in. No letters changed hands and nothing was placed on my record. The innocent minor infractions of a civilian about to join the Army are of little or no importance to the military hierarchy. But it was an abrupt, unexpected lesson that I never forgot—Be careful. The system has been established over the years by custom and written regulation. Do not buck it.

I learned the lesson in the Federal Building in Chicago and I relearned it with every phase of the military life I experienced. Everyone in the military establishment has a boss. I started out with upper classmen bossing me around. And I had flight instructors, tactical officers and layers upon layers of officers up the line. Even after the promotions of my career, even though I became a boss, I always had a superior officer to whom I answered. True in every walk of life, yes, but particularly true in military organizations. Discipline here is more formal and pronounced. The intention is not to stymie progress or personal initiative but to ensure that the man in charge has his instructions carried out, that he knows the status of his operation and that he maintains personal control.

I knew this literally from day one, hour one. Now don't you suppose that the Big Boss, General of the Armies Douglas MacArthur, was aware of this basic military principal?

You bet he was. He told his wartime physician that a soldier's loyalty was the most important quality in his character—loyalty up and loyalty down. Yet it was necessary that the President advise him publicly, "Full and vigorous debate on matters of national policy is a vital element in the constitutional system of our free democracy. It is fundamental, however, that military commanders must be governed by the policies and directives issued to them in the manner provided by our laws and constitution."

Did his ego dictate that this policy did not apply to him? What was in his mind? Few know. Even with all the authority given to him as Commander of American and United Nations military forces in the Far East and the occupation forces in Japan, he answered to the Joint Chiefs of Staff and to his Commander-in-Chief Harry S. Truman. Yes, even a five-star General is accountable, to his liking or not.

General MacArthur certainly knew his line of command. He had the background, the training, the intelligence and the experience to know that primary code. He was born into a military family. Most all his education was in the military. His entire working career was in the military, a long and very distinguished career, as was his father's before him.

What happened in his head when China came to the defense of North Korea? Many have tried to analyze the situation and as many opinions have been offered as there are analyzers. One wag stated that the General always tended to be independent and overbearing and had been free to be so until he ran into Harry Truman. Harry Truman, a man of stronger will and conviction than the General perceived, in an office that determines policy for the United States of America. "In America," Truman emphasized, "it is the President who makes decisions."

Beyond the personalities of the two men were their views. MacArthur, the warrior, number one man in the field, victorious hero, wanted to win this battle as he determined to win every battle. Truman, his Commander-in-Chief, did not want to risk becoming engaged in an expanded war with the Chinese and potentially the Russians. The buck stopped with Truman, who as both President of the people and Commander of the military, sought an economical victory without exploding the conflict into global warfare.

The impasse was inevitable.

The hard, simple fact was that Truman was MacArthur's boss. When you don't agree with your boss you come to an understanding that settles the differences. Or you quit.

But MacArthur could not bring himself to comply with distasteful orders from a higher source. He could not subject himself to the establishment. Nor could he quit.

So on April 10, 1951, the Commander-in-Chief relieved and replaced the five star general with this explanation: With deep regret I have concluded that General of the Army Douglas MacArthur is unable to give his wholehearted support to the policies of the United States government and of the United Nations . . .

He had no other choice.

I was in that war, too, now as Commanding General of the U.S. Air Force 315th Air Division in charge of all intra-theater transports. Through the Fifth Air Force, we worked at the United Nation's direction.

This firing was a bomb dropped on me and my associates who were sorry to realize how matters had deteriorated. We were in the midst of serious conflict and since "the war must go on," it did.

A couple of days after the explosive demotion, I and all general officers received an official communique from headquarters inviting us, "so far as our duties would permit," to bid General and Mrs. MacArthur farewell at Haneda Air Base, April 16, 1951. We were to be in place at 7 a.m.

Headquarters for my 315th Air Division were at Fuchu, near the town of Koganei, an immediate suburb west of Tokyo where I lived. To guarantee my being in place at seven, I drove into Tokyo the evening before, staying at the Imperial Hotel, only 15 or 20 minutes away from Haneda.

The Imperial Hotel is on a street that intersects the road to the base leading from MacArthur's residence, the imposing mansion of the former U.S. Ambassador. My driver was moving my car down that street by 6 a.m. We knew we were on the right path when we happened on it. The road was blocked off. We were permitted to enter and proceed only because we were in an official Air Force blue staff vehicle.

Few of the two million sightseers to later line the road for a glimpse of the MacArthurs had come at that early hour. More impressive was the honor guard of 10,000 dark blue uniformed Japanese policemen and security forces marking the route, standing alert, still and quiet every few paces on either side of the road, two silent lines stretching seven miles from Tokyo to Haneda as early morning light punctured the quiet, hazy view.

We saw the newly renamed "Bataan" through the mist when we reached the NATS (Naval Air Transport Service) terminal. The General's beloved, magnificent four engine, triple tailed Constellation, Lockheed's elegant plane that had carried him from Wake Island, from Korea, from Honolulu . . . was standing a couple of hundred yards beyond the building.

I greeted Colonel Tony Story, the General's Air Force aide and pilot. He had just filed his flight plan to carry the General away from Japan, back to the land he had not set foot on in fourteen years. The weather looked good to him all the way to Pearl Harbor's Hickam Air Base. He expected only one refueling stop.

The farewell ceremony for General MacArthur, Commander of American and United Nations Military Forces in the Far East, April 16, 1951, after he was relieved of his duty by President Truman.

Per instructions, the general officers and other military present began lining the right side of the passageway to the entrance ramp leading to the passenger door at the left rear of the Connie.

Opposite this military lineup were about a hundred civilians, diplomats, dependents, civil servants and friends who were serving in Japan during the MacArthur reign.

At the entrance to the ceremony area, near the base operations building and opposite the airplane, were a military band and an honor guard composed of a platoon from each service, Army, Navy, Air Force and Marines.

It was 7 a.m. Everyone was in place. At that moment a large black four-door limousine arrived at the ceremony area entrance, an assistant opened the right rear door and he emerged. An Army commander of the honor guard saluted and greeted the former SCAP. MacArthur, 71 years old, sharply returned the hand salute and stood at attention, with the honor guard, with all the military personnel, with all the civilians, while the band played "Ruffles and Flourishes," the age-old military musical salute accorded dignitaries.

The showman was center stage again. The music of the band filled the cool early morning. He was dressed in a long khaki trench coat characteristically buttoned at the top and casually tied around the waist by a buckleless belt and of course that braided cap he had made famous. He stood motionless.

When the music ended, accompanied only by the commander, he reviewed the honor guard. He did not break the rhythm of his pace with questions or with chitchat. He kept the symbolism intact. He was not inspecting but reviewing. Had it been an inspection, though, he would not have found a fault. Not a button nor cap out of place. The guard was totally "spit and polish."

Watching the General "troop the line" is watching exquisite choreography. His dress, his stride, his military bearing, his hint of a swagger, his timing—it is an unforgettable image. He moved sharply down the full length of the guard, returned to the center front with the commander where they saluted and shook hands.

The General moved to the center of the lined passageway where he was joined by Mrs. MacArthur. Together they walked down the left side to greet, shake hands, say farewell or embrace the many friends they had cultivated over their five and a half years in Tokyo. The process of goodbye was casual, unhurried and sincere. Occasionally emotions erupted.

After these personal farewells, the General and his wife moved along the passageway to the head of our military formation nearest the honor guard. MacArthur, followed by Mrs. MacArthur, proceeded along this rigid line, each of us standing at attention. He shook every hand. He had no personal words for any of us. To each of us he said "Thank you" or "Thank you very much" or "Thank you and goodbye." No one saluted.

The petite Mrs. MacArthur followed after the General, warmly greeting everyone, looking each of us in the eye. She was attractive and friendly, with an engaging personality. She shook our hands with such warmth we felt she had been and would be a friend for life.

The departing couple worked its way to the beginning of the line where a mobile stairway led up to the passenger door of the Connie. He paused at the bottom step while she preceded him to the platform outside the door. When he arrived to stand next to her they both turned to wave goodbye.

Then, out of the hazy silence rang a loud and vigorous "banzai" from the

General and Mrs. MacArthur wave goodbye on departing from Japan

Japanese prime minister and his score of ministers and political leaders gathered at the foot of the mobile stairs. Banzai—the traditional Japanese wish of "ten thousand years"—was coming from the conquered to the man who had won them over ultimately with his sincerity, efficiency, honesty and style.

To that moment, the General and his wife had been holding their emotions in check. The music, the military grandeur, the throngs of friends and cohorts—they had absorbed it all with cool detachment. Until "banzai" burst from the crowd. Overtaken with sentiment, Mrs. MacArthur tried to salvage her composure and wave one last time but could not. She turned weeping and entered the plane to join her son and staff.

The General, still standing as shocked, respectful, then warm applause washed over the Japanese cheer, stoically waved once more, turned and passed through the door.

The door closed on an era.

John Henebry in New Guinea, 1943

Rank and medals of John Henebry

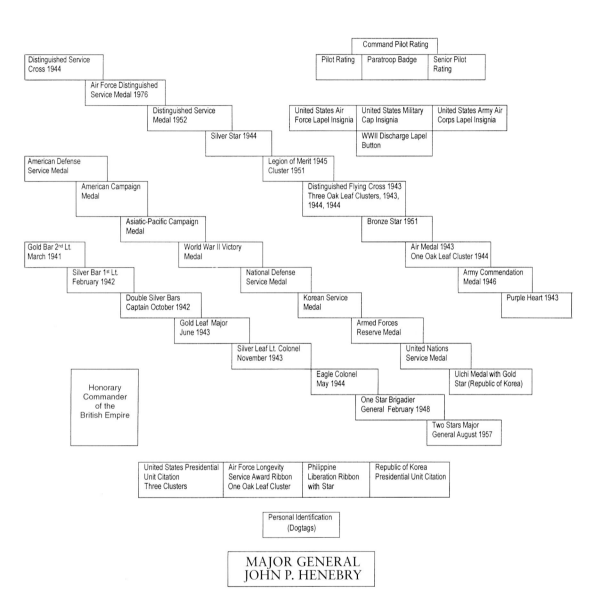

Command Pilot Rating

| Pilot Rating | Paratroop Badge | Senior Pilot Rating |

Distinguished Service Cross 1944

Air Force Distinguished Service Medal 1976

Distinguished Service Medal 1952

| United States Air Force Lapel Insignia | United States Military Cap Insignia | United States Army Air Corps Lapel Insignia |
| | WWII Discharge Lapel Button | |

Silver Star 1944

Legion of Merit 1945 Cluster 1951

American Defense Service Medal

American Campaign Medal

Distinguished Flying Cross 1943 Three Oak Leaf Clusters, 1943, 1944, 1944

Asiatic-Pacific Campaign Medal

Bronze Star 1951

Gold Bar 2nd Lt. March 1941

World War II Victory Medal

Air Medal 1943 One Oak Leaf Cluster 1944

Silver Bar 1st Lt. February 1942

National Defense Service Medal

Army Commendation Medal 1946

Double Silver Bars Captain October 1942

Korean Service Medal

Purple Heart 1943

Gold Leaf Major June 1943

Armed Forces Reserve Medal

Silver Leaf Lt. Colonel November 1943

United Nations Service Medal

Eagle Colonel May 1944

Ulchi Medal with Gold Star (Republic of Korea)

Honorary Commander of the British Empire

One Star Brigadier General February 1948

Two Stars Major General August 1957

| United States Presidential Unit Citation Three Clusters | Air Force Longevity Service Award Ribbon One Oak Leaf Cluster | Philippine Liberation Ribbon with Star | Republic of Korea Presidential Unit Citation |

Personal Identification (Dogtags)

MAJOR GENERAL
JOHN P. HENEBRY

Key to rank and medals

John Henebry at retirement as Major General, 1976